# Jack's Drift

# Jack's Drift

## J. Wilfred Cahill

authorHOUSE®

*AuthorHouse*™
*1663 Liberty Drive*
*Bloomington, IN 47403*
*www.authorhouse.com*
*Phone: 1-800-839-8640*

*First published by AuthorHouse 09/28/2011*

*ISBN: 978-1-4567-6530-9 (sc)*
*ISBN: 978-1-4567-6529-3 (hc)*
*ISBN: 978-1-4567-6528-6 (ebk)*

*Library of Congress Control Number: 2011907417*

*Front cover photo: Gunnison River, Colorado*
*Back cover Photo: Shelter Creek, Alaska*
*Photos by J. Wilfred Cahill*

*Printed in the United States of America*

# Contents

Dedication ............................................................vii

Sentiment...........................................................ix

Forward.............................................................xi

Rigging ..............................................................1

Drift 1    Oh! Black Water ...................................5

Drift 2    Volcano Chicken ..................................18

Drift 3    Ssss .....................................................26

Drift 4    For the Birds........................................33

Drift 5    The Black Vole .....................................45

Drift 6    Pay your money and take your chances.........49

Drift 7    Gabby's Dilemma ................................60

Drift 8    Rocky and Bullwinkle...........................68

Drift 9    Wha'd he take?.....................................75

Drift 10   Her Stinky Beaver................................86

Drift 11   The Gau Lieter of Nellie Martin ............93

Drift 12   The View From Abaft...........................108

Drift 13   Bubba's Chub ......................................118

Drift 14   Naps ...................................................127

Drift 15   New Guy(How Stumpy Got His Name)......137

Drift 16   There's a lot of waiting when you're a dog......150

Drift 17   The Big Two-Hearted Dutchman ...........156

Drift 18   Parshall Red Tide.................................167

Drift 19   Net Boy ..........................................................173

Drift 20   The Last Cast ...............................................184


Reeling In ....................................................................190

About the Author .........................................................192

# Dedication

For Jack
Thanks, Daddy

# Sentiment

I can thank only heaven that as a young man,
I thought I knew everything.
Or I would have feared to try anything.
As a mature man who has tried everything
I am relieved to be shed of the burden such knowledge is.

# forward

*Cahill and I literally met in another life and reunited in this one by a throw of the dice. I know and this is how. In the early 1970's I was sent on a Coast Guard rescue mission 140 miles south of Cameron, LA.; into the middle of the Gulf of Mexico. We met on that rescue but didn't know it. Although he was not the subject; he was present. We met officially in 1992 by a chance visit to his office in Carbondale, Colorado. Ten years later he co-authored the book on my Coast Guard life. A year later he told me of a Coast Guard helicopter rescue he witnessed while building off shore drilling platforms in the Gulf of Mexico. The story haunted me because it sounded like so many I had flown during my aviation career yet gave me a distinct feeling of recollection. He mentioned it again some months later, before I left on a trip for New Orleans, suggesting I might look into it at the Coast Guard archives. Just out of curiosity I pulled out my old flight logs from my tenure as a Coast Guard aviator there. I was astounded to find the exact mission he described entered in my own hand all those years before. Suddenly our relationship assumed a whole new dimension.*

*Jack's Drift isn't just a collection of fishing stories from a Master Fisherman, but it is also a look into one man's soul related through an almost religious respect for life, then translated through a language that only fishermen speak and everyone understands. This book is no more about Trout fishing than "The Old Man of the Sea" is a story about Marlin. So, put on your waders, grab your belly-boats and float back with him in time to those spots in your own memories that bring big smiles as well as tears. This book will make you feel good. Cahill uses his love for fly fishing as the thread through his life experiences that brought him from childhood to this time in his life, that is gifted with his grandson and his memories. Jack his father and Jack his grandson are linked through a series fishing experiences that we can connect with emotionally, and even spiritually. His irreverent sense of humor and his grip on reality will make you laugh and cry in the same paragraph.*

*Cahill is considered one of the most talented and knowledgeable fly fisherman on the Western Slope of Colorado. He could have taken another path and followed the career of a highly successful commercial fly fishing guide. But that would have entailed an act of near prostitution; receiving money for his love. It also would have transformed him from the eccentric purist in a faded, somewhat soiled and tattered baseball cap, a t-shirt of unknown vintage, an outer shirt worn at the elbows with more patches than original material, and trousers that can stand up in the corner by themselves, into something unacceptable to him.*

*As a person, he is a mixture of John Wayne and Felix Unger. He never does anything half way, except perhaps in sticking to the scheduling of the rest of his life. He will drop anything in an instant to go fishing, and then re-schedule everything else for a later date.*

*From a marine rigger building oil platforms in the Gulf of Mexico to a Wall St. banker, to hitchhiking with his guitar to Aspen, Colorado, he has grown into a man of character. He's a guy who will stand shoulder to shoulder with you in some cowboy bar in the Rockies facing down too many antagonists, knowing that the two of you are probably going to have your bell rung-but with no regrets. Then, over coffee the next morning, he'll wax poetic about the joy a fishing life has brought.*

*Enjoy JACK'S DRIFT and enjoy J. Wilfred Cahill. They're page-turners.*

*LCDR Malcolm R. Smith (USCG Retired)*
*Aviator/Author/Speaker/Teller of Tales*

# Rigging

Grampa Cahill, John Joseph, was a Wall St. banker. Everyone called him "Deedy". Grampa Bourgeois, Wilfred, was a New England house painter. Everyone called him "Pip".

Deedy always said, "The only thing you can control in this life is the tool in your hand at that moment". Pip always told me, "Put some paint on that brush son. You're rubbing it on". They were both right. I am their name sake.

When I was twelve my father took me to the garage where he picked up a paint brush and a fly rod.

"First I'll teach you to use this," he said extending the hand with the paint brush. "When the house is painted I'll teach you to use this," he said, waving the fly rod. I can paint really fast now.

I finally took that proffered fly rod from his hand on some small and long forgotten creek in the Wasatch Mountains of Utah. I have been a fly fisherman ever since. I am mesmerized by water.

Through the years of fly fishing, certain things have happened while doing it that struck me as funny, poignant, amazing and scary. At some point I felt compelled to write about it. When I researched what to do with such writings, I was aghast to find that publishers where not interested in what I had so diligently composed. They did not accept "Me & Joe" stories. I understood. I got serious and even wrote to the publisher of Fly Fishing magazine about it. He replied with a lovely note, encouraging me to submit. I tried to write within the accepted format, but I couldn't bring myself to compose satisfactorily about tying a "Sprattle Legged Geezul Bug". I never use them. Nor did I care to write about where to fish. Why would I divulge my favorite spots to the general public? I only show my closest buddies if they are willing to take an oath on their best rod. I do make their dogs exempt; dogs do not talk about such things. I didn't know anything about rod building and I still don't. I found the subjects of reels, lines and casting infinitely boring. The selection of flies seemed an endless and inconclusive topic. I mean really—how many are there anyway? When I look at the bins in any fly shop, my eyes cross.

I like Me & Joe. We've had some wonderful times together and shared superior fishing. Me & Joe are experienced, knowledgeable and dedicated fly fisherman. We operate under a specific code of conduct. We observe the proprieties, like not donning one's fishing attire while the vehicle is still in motion, thus gaining unfair advantage over our companion(s). We are model fly fishermen.

OK then, Me & Joe it would be. Joe could represent every angling partner I have had, despite their real names. I am sure some of them would not relish mention in any book, considering what they may have done or at least been party to. The concept relieved me of any angst about telling what really happened. I could offend no one and still tell the horrible truth. I loved it.

As I thought on, I realized the name Joe wasn't quite right. Again I struggled. This writing thing isn't for sissies. It takes some effort and commitment. Then I remembered my first and best fishing buddy. He would not mind if I used his name. It was Jack. He was my dad. After all, it was Jack who first let me feel the magic in a fly rod. It was he who took me to all those wonderful places and carried my gear. It was Jack who rigged my rod and untangled my bird nests. Joe never did such things for me.

Even in the years after our lives were separated by half a continent, we continued to fish together. We did so over the telephone or through pictures I sent him. In my fortieth year I realized how important he was to me, and began to call him almost every night. I usually did this while preparing the family dinner. For, after almost twenty years of marriage, my bride had decided it was my turn and assigned the task to me. I took the assignment with great enthusiasm, as it provided the opportunity to chat with Jack while I fiddled in the kitchen. Most nights, with time zones and caller ID in his favor, he answered with a hearty, "You're late." We talked about our individual days, his maladies, mom's maladies, but always the topic turned to fishing. Although we had only fished together two or three times since I left home—we fished almost every night on the telephone.

Jack it would be then. Jack would be my Joe.

# Drift 1

# Oh! Black Water

Every summer during my early childhood on Long Island, Jack drove the family for a visit to my mother's childhood home in Bennington, Vermont. He also had relatives on his mother's side in Burlington. In fact he attended St. Michael's College in Burlington, which is where he met mom. Mom's side of the family was of French Canadian descent. They were Wilfred and Elise Bourgeois—Mim and Pip.

The first night at Mim and Pip's was exciting. They put on a big feast. All the aunts and uncles attended. Because mom was one of twelve children, the little house on Division Street was packed to the rafters once all arrived with spouses and children (my cousins) in tow. During the consternation of arrivals and greetings, Pip took me to the basement of the little dwelling to drink homemade root beer while I watched, fascinated, as he made fishing lures from old spoons. He ground and filed them to the desired shape. When he was satisfied, he drilled holes in either end before painting them and/or attaching feathers. The final step was attaching the treble hook to one end and a swivel to the other.

I thought he made these lures because he was poor and could not afford the ready-made kind. After all, he had raised twelve children, and there were many grandchildren (my cousins again) to care about. In fact his friends called him "Budget—Budget Bougie"; because he was always on one. But he made the lures because he enjoyed it, and they worked better than anything he could buy. I have discovered over the years that nothing is more satisfying than catching something on a fly or lure you have created. I think Pip knew this well. Besides, Pip was not a catch and release fisherman. I don't know if the concept even existed in the mid 1950's. If so, it was not practiced by hard bitten Vermont fisherman with twelve children to feed. I am sure he fed his family often from the waters in the Green Mountain Forest around Bennington—the budget again.

When he finished the lure and I had consumed my fill of root beer (Pip made the best root beer), we ascended to the festivities, where he announced how much I had enjoyed the soda. Mim, of course, gave him a perfunctory scolding for allowing me a treat so close to dinner. She also added a stern word about making lures from any of her good spoons.

On one such visit, a rental cabin awaited us on the shores of Lake Champlain. Pip came along. The cabin was perched on a low bluff above the lake's black rock beach, where a wood dock berthed an old lap strake skiff with a small outboard motor. A set of wooden stairs led down the bluff to the dock. The skiff had seen better days, but she was still lake worthy, all sixteen feet of her. She boasted triple thwarts, well worn oars, and a leaky bottom. The outboard looked more like an abused and retrofitted kitchen mixer, but it ran well and pushed the little craft across the lake with ease.

The first morning, Jack and Pip rose early to prepare the lunch, load the gear and make the skiff ready for a day on the lake. The weather was very cool and a mist hung low over the water. From atop the bluff I could barely see them on the dock. I ran down the stairs and across the stone beach. The water was like a great pool of ink—motionless.

"Where's your jacket?" Jack demanded.

"I'm not cold." I gave my usual reply.

"You will be. Go get it," he insisted.

I ran the length of the dock back towards the stairs.

"Don't run!" they both yelled in unison.

I slowed for a few steps, but regained full tilt by the time I burst through the cabin door, with mom yelling in my passage to slow down. I couldn't. I was too excited. Descending the stairs 2 at a time, I emerged from the mist onto the beach. I raced across it, catching my foot on the edge of the dock. I stumbled and rolled the length of it, coming to rest against Jack's feet. If not for his stance I would have continued into the lake. Jacket in hand, I stepped aboard and took the center thwart. Jack cranked the little outboard several times and fussed with the choke between each pull until it sputtered to life. We were off.

I loved gliding along in that little skiff and could not resist dragging my hand in the indigo of the lake's surface as Jack let Pip navigate him to a little cove about ½ hour from the dock. Soon the breeze created by the forward motion of the craft, coupled with the rate of evaporation off my hand and wrist, brought on a mighty shiver. Jack was right. I put on the jacket and hunkered down below the gunnels-ass on the ribs just out of the bilge. I was cold and dangerously close to being wet. The mist seemed only inches over my head, because it was. If this was fishing, it sucked. I wanted to go home already. Not just back to the cabin, but all the way home to Long Island. They both shook their heads at my obvious discomfort.

After what seemed a lifetime to a miserable 7-year-old, Jack steered the little skiff into a small cove. He cut the motor at the entry and glided silently into its middle. Pip gently lowered the anchor.

"I'm cold," I whined loudly, hoping the volume of my complaint would change something—anything.

"Sshh—you'll scare the fish," they hushed.

They started to fish. I stayed hunkered and miserable, shivering in the bottom of the old skiff. Little by little the sun cut through the morning mist. I felt it begin to take the chill from me, and soon I felt warm enough to place my hands on the wet gunnels and peer over the top. As I did, Jack was retrieving one of Pip's specials. A fish hit the lure hard and his rod bent at the tip. Jack skipped it across the surface. Seconds into his retrieval, the water behind the little pan fish began to roil. Suddenly, the fish disappeared into the gaping maw of a very large Pike, its mouth so large, a cereal box could have stood within it. The big fish realized something was pulling on its breakfast and for a few seconds the water at the end of Jack's line churned to a froth.

Jack jerked. The smaller fish disappeared into the depths of both the lake and the pike. Line, lure and small pieces of fish lips piled back against his chest. Suddenly I was warm. I grabbed the kid's spinning rod leaning against the gunnels, rigged with one of Pip's specials. Regaining the center thwart, I cast as taught. Within a few casts I was on. My first fish was on the stringer. The jacket came off with a tug. All thoughts of home vanished from my mind. I could think of only one thing—the next fish.

To this day, when I stand beside some river or on a lake, I always hear the sputter of that little outboard. I can feel the black silky water of Lake Champlain and remember the big one that got away. I always have a jacket in my pack.

In all honesty, I cannot recall much more about fishing until the family moved to Salt Lake City when I was about twelve. By that time I had a little sister and brother. It was difficult for Jack to take much time, and fishing was something that became a special treat for him, as it was for me. When he did manage to go I always went along. The other kids were too young. Those times stand out in memory because it was only me and Jack.

At our previous home in Buffalo, Jack had taught me to ski. This made Salt Lake a paradise for us. Ski areas like Alta, Brighton and Solitude were just minutes away from the house. Park City was the beginning of someone's dream. We skied it when there was only one chairlift. The alluring Uintah and Wasatch Mountains were close by. They are rife with lakes and streams, especially the north slope of those ranges. We scoured the little streams that ran down from Big and Little

Cottonwood canyons, at whose tops stood the ski areas. We took the summer chairlift at Brighton to the top and hiked to a lake called St. Mary's. It was there along those boulder strewn shores that I caught my first truly big Rainbow. It was a monster that fed the whole family dinner that very night. Catch and release was an unknown concept to us back then.

And so it was that Jack and I began our adventures with rod and reel. We fished a lake that was miles off the main road in south central Utah. It took what seemed endless hours of jostling travel over dirt canyon land roads to reach it. We tent camped out of the family station wagon. Although the spot was scenic and well forested, the lake was disappointing. It is obvious to me now that it was an irrigation impoundment. From the high water mark to the water itself, a wide mud flat kept us from reaching the water's edge. It was not fishable.

Jack would not be dissuaded, despite his failure to purchase cigarettes when we provisioned ourselves before leaving the pavement. Even in the throes of nicotine withdrawal he persisted. He led me along the high water mark to a small feeder creek. The boulder strewn rivulet was difficult to negotiate, but along its winding course good pocket water abounded. There was just enough room to work a rod. Not far upstream, Jack found a water-logged pack of Camel straights. As I came upon him, he was gently unwrapping the sodden find and laying the individual cigarettes, now brown with tobacco stain, on a large flat boulder to dry in the searing Utah sun. He stood guard over them and fished the pocket water adjacent to the rock while they dried, and caught several nice trout for his patience. Years later, when recalling the trip, he always proclaimed how "those saved my ass." We fished the creek for another day before the Camels ran out and his craving finally overcame his desire to fish. We caught many fish those two days.

We took a trip together to Lake Powell. In the early 1960's the lake was just beginning to fill after the completion of Glen Canyon Dam. In those days it was called Glen Canyon Reservoir. Jack drove the dirt roads of the canyon lands over mesas and through washes, only to come to an abrupt end where the road dove into the newly rising lake. Some roads reappeared down the shore within our sight, but there was simply no way to reach them. In most instances we parked right there and fished. It fished well. We camped among the cedars and pinions out of the faithful and reliable old station wagon, and slept in his umbrella tent. On the second or third day, we woke to find the tent ceiling just inches above our noses and water dripping profusely through it. Outside we found the tent had nearly collapsed under the weight of a foot of heavy, wet June snow. We spent a sodden, chilly morning preparing breakfast and breaking camp in the snow and muck. The rest of the day was consumed with crawling back to the pavement. I don't think I have ever been so glad to end a fishing trip.

The Uintah Mountains were always one of Jack's favorite areas to fish and camp. We spent a great deal of time there. On our return from a trip to Mirror Lake in the high Uintah, we stopped at a spot Jack had heard about called Alexander Lake. It was a remarkable place. Alexander was surrounded by a wide flat of floating tundra-like vegetation. Crossing it was necessary to reach the open water. Jack tested it with a tentative step. The entire mass undulated under his weight and sent a ripple across the open water, but he found that if he kept moving it would support him. The trick was not to stand in the same spot too long. If he did, he slowly began to sink. He cautioned me to follow but not to step in his tracks. I was so nervous about sinking through that fishing was the last thing on my mind, but I timidly followed his lead. The tundra undulated even more with both of us plodding across it. It was the spookiest thing I have ever done, not counting fishing next to bears in Alaska. I fished by casting the lure a goodly distance out and walking along the edge of the tundra, dragging the lure through the water as I took tiny steps along the floating mass. I just didn't want to sink. I didn't crank the reel until I had finally walked far enough to bring the lure in parallel with the tundra's edge. That's when I caught the first fish. From that point on I simply cast the lure along the edge of the mass and walked, pulling the lure along. Jack saw what I was doing and imitated my technique. We began to catch some fish as we danced the "no sink two step".

Our agony and ecstasy were sharply ended when the leader of a troop of Scouts, camped by the lake, called anxiously from the dry land side of the tundra for Jack to come. We carefully made our way back to hard ground. The Scoutmaster explained that, while felling a large dead standing tree for firewood, one of the scouts had been injured when a big dead limb fell, striking him on the head. Since the Scoutmaster needed to attend the injured lad and the scouts could not drive, he asked Jack to go for help. We left immediately. Jack stopped at the first pay phone he could find and called the cops. I don't know what happened to the scout, but we never paid a visit to Alexander Lake again.

Somewhere in all the river and stream traipsing, Jack bought a broom handle fly rod and automatic reel. I was twelve. The reel was mounted side saddle, giving the rig an odd and futuristic look. Jack was always a sucker for any gadget. We practiced in the yard with it for hours. Our first trip with the new fly rod was life-changing for me. One day he used the rod on a small stream in the Wasatch for a few hours, and then asked me if I wanted to try it. Of course I did.

My only problem with the new fly rod was the stream itself. It was bush and tree lined. My first back cast snagged the limbs behind me, and of course I snapped the fly off trying to jerk it loose from the limbs high over my head. I did the same with the next fly. He came to my aid by pulling the overhanging limb down to enable him to reach it. He took the rod from my hands and showed me the roll cast.

I hadn't seen this technique before. He'd been holding out on me. All the practice had made me familiar enough with the mechanics of a fly rod that I was easily able to pick up the roll cast. Soon I was catching fish. I was a fly fisherman. Poor Jack rarely used the fly rod thereafter. For the remainder of our time in Utah it was my rod.

In my sophomore year of high school the family moved to St. Paul and sadly, fishing was over for awhile. In my senior year the family moved again, to an old country farmhouse outside Bel Air, Maryland. By a quirk of fate, one of my classmates was an avid fisherman. He introduced me to Shad fishing on the Susquehanna River below the Conowingo Dam, at the very headwaters of Chesapeake Bay. We also fished the numerous farm ponds and small lakes that dot the countryside of northeastern Maryland, for Bass, Crappie and Bluegill. But the Shad fishing was the most fun.

Shad are not a good eating fish, and most of the local anglers harvested them for the roe, which is considered a delicacy. I didn't get it, and my interest lay in the fact that they are an excellent game fish. A Shad bent on completing its' spawning run will rip even the most seasoned angler.

I took Jack out once during that time. But the aspects of Shad fishing on the Susquehanna River across from Havre de Grace, Maryland were more than he could tolerate. It was serious elbow to elbow combat fishing, with the anglers in deep competition. It rankled many of the local roe harvesters to see me put a big female bulging with eggs back in the water. I usually excused my cultural faux pas by suggesting they were free to catch it again.

"I just put it back out there for you."

It was not until later, when I moved to Aspen and started my own family, that I was able to rekindle my old flame. The pilot to that furnace was well primed and the burner easily lit. I lived in the heart of the central Rockies where I could walk to world class fishing.

Of course, by then the old broom handle and auto-reel were long gone, and even Jack had no clue to what had become of them. If I were to fly fish, I needed a rig. I found an old and bent Martin #65 fly reel that someone had discarded—complete with line and leader. I managed to purchase my own broom handle at the local variety store. It set me back $8. At the time, coming up with the eight bucks was a serious stretch of our budget. Flies were another financing problem altogether, but finally despite rent, car payment and diapers, I was able to put a small box together. I scrounged a pair of old, leaky hip waders from the local thrift shop, along with a used suit vest. I slit the inside liner of the vest and hemmed the open edges with duct tape for pockets large enough to hold fly boxes and the other accoutrements of the sport—voila, fishing vest. I must have looked quite the sight to the more elegantly equipped I encountered on the river. The fish, however, did not seem to mind. The old skill came back like riding a bike

When my daughter turned two, we moved from Aspen to the top of the Frying Pan River. The place was called De Haven Ranch. It was a former Christian boys' camp with a five-bedroom main house and 15 cabins, located on the confluence of the North and South forks of that legendary trout stream. We rented the cabins to hard rock miners building the water diversion tunnels of the Pan-Ark water project, which took excess stream flows from the western slope of the Rockies to the eastern slope. The rents brought in just enough to pay the ranch lease and buy the groceries. I supplemented our income by building custom furniture for the affluent second-home owners in Aspen. When I wasn't collecting rent, repairing cabins or building furniture, I had only yards to walk to either fork of the Frying Pan River.

Many mornings I was on the river by sunrise and home with my limit by breakfast time. Hey! I was supplementing. I had a family to feed. Some days, when I didn't have time for the river, I caught fish with my hands out of the irrigation ditch running through the property. It's not as hard as it sounds.

The best parts about De Haven were the 27 mile isolation from town, the rapture of living in the wilderness, the ease with which we earned our living, and the times I could take my toddler fishing. I carried her in one of those aluminum frame back packs that were so popular among parents in the 1970's. While she talked, watched and napped, I fished. I can draw a detailed map of every pool, rock or run on that stretch of river, between the confluences and Horseshoe Bend Guest Ranch. We fished it that much. It is a beautiful section of river. There is some magic there.

Late one afternoon in the summer of 1977, my toddling daughter was cranky and wholly out of sorts. She would not hear of taking a nap. Any efforts to put her down only exacerbated her grump. So, at my bride's behest, I put down my planes and chisels to take the kid fishing. I loaded her in the back pack and headed out the front door. It was great that I could actually stop work and go fishing any time I cared to. She was out cold, in a full drool with her head on my shoulder, before I made the quarter mile walk to the South Fork. I fished for an hour or so, consistently stepping upriver between casts to keep some lulling motion going—like a cradle. Every parent knows the quickest way to put a kid to sleep is to load them in the car and drive around the block, and the back pack worked much the same way. In fact, I sometimes put her in it while I worked in the furniture shop. She would sleep soundly under the rhythm of a hand plane or saw. I never used a power tool while she was on my back, but I did hold her in my lap while I ran the old TD-6 International bulldozer, which served as a snow plow during the winter. The bulldozer and 2 feet of snow every week were a Godsend to the sanity of young parents. Fishing was tough in the winter, even if you could find the river.

This day she woke, as all kids eventually do, so I left the ankle-deep slack water to find a suitable spot to let her out of the pack for a while. We sat on the grassy bank, had a drink and watched birds. I skipped rocks for her. When time came to go, I grabbed the pack. As I started to don it she said:

"John, I want to wear my pack."

She called me John back then. It seemed OK to me. I had just carried her for more than a mile while trying to remain upright on rocks that were well greased with river moss and slime. She could walk for a while. I cinched up the shoulder straps on the pack to fit her tiny frame and put it on her. When I took her little hand in mine to begin the walk home, she looked up at me with the most angelic face, painted in utter sincerity, and said:

"OK, John, get in."

I don't recall the fish, if any, or the flies I used. Only her words have stuck in my memory all these years. It may have been the best fishing day ever. I owe that day to Jack.

The funny thing is that she called me John and I called him Jack.

# Drift 2

# Volcano Chicken

Many a greasy breakfast has been gobbled at restaurants, campsites and pickup tailgates. I have eaten more mashed or extruded sandwiches than a man should ever possess; some soggy ones as well, chips that were reduced to powder, and candy bars that had to be drunk after spending the day cooking inside a pack left in the sun. But none of it prepared me for the evening meal with Jack on the North Fork of the Gunnison after fishing a place called "Mike's."

A river that we had neglected over twenty years, driving by it to the better known waters of southern Colorado, the Gunnison, Rio Grande and Conejos, because it ran dirty most every time I saw it, and because I had never seen any fisherman along it. We tried it en route to the Kokanee run around Almont, Colorado. It was on our way.

Jack is not a fan of extravagant camp cuisine. It takes too much time and he likes to fish until absolute dark. By the time gear is put up, a fire started, and cocktails had, there just isn't much time left for culinary fol-de-rol. Hence, the menu is usually set by him and often includes some type of boil in the bag, freeze-dried, or otherwise pre-prepared fare. Sometimes we eat in restaurants before heading to a campsite, sometimes we take the meal to go and dine at whatever site is close and accessible. I do insist that he let me enjoy a hearty breakfast at a restaurant, if one is nearby our camp or on the way to the next fishing spot.

We set a date and agreed to provide our own fried chicken for the evening meal at Erickson Springs campground on Anthracite Creek. Jack prefers fried chicken. With fried chicken there is no prep time, no dishes to wash, and the remnants can be disposed of in the evening fire. It could, I guess, be considered a green dinner, as minimal carbon footprint is left by the camper. The chicken might see it another way.

At the time a road improvement project was under way along the stretch we called Mike's and the access points were in the work zone. Mike's is so named for a little cabin just feet off the highway which had a sign above the front door proclaiming it, "Mike's". Upstream from the little cabin is a Colorado Department of Transportation work yard with a magnificent log cabin, (for plow drivers I think—it's at the very bottom of McClure Pass). Upstream is the public access to the very beginning of the North Fork of the Gunnison. In the confusion caused by all the road work, we turned into the DOT work yard and parked our trucks at the very back, right on the river.

It was late in the afternoon with only a few hours of daylight left for fishing. We began the ritual of donning our fishing attire and rigging rods. Jack munched a piece of fried chicken while pulling his waders on.

"I hope you brought some extra chicken, Cahill. I've kinda' been eating this the whole way over here," he said.

I assured him that I had, so he offered me the last piece of his stash. I happily took it, knowing I had plenty for our evening meal and probably enough for lunch the next day. While this transpired, a paving contractor's pickup rolled up to us. Immediately I stepped up to greet the driver, waving Jack's last chicken leg in the air.

"Is it OK to fish here?" I asked, as I approached the truck; hoping the answer would be yes.

"Got any more of that chicken?" he replied.

"Sure," I responded enthusiastically and reached in my cooler for a big breast. I handed it to him through the open cab window.

"Thanks. It's OK for you guys to fish here, but the public access is about 200 yards upstream—'tother side of that cabin." He pointed with the chicken breast.

We thanked him through chicken-stuffed mouths and he was on his way. Jack grilled me again about having enough chicken for dinner and giving it away so casually. I assured him I had a big bag in the cooler. We continued our rigging and finally stepped into the water next to our trucks. The second I wet my boots, an empty dump truck from the same company roared up to the spot between our trucks and skidded to a stop, momentarily swathing us in a cloud of dust and diesel exhaust. As the cloud cleared, I could see the driver jerking his thumb over his shoulder and yelling, over the idling clatter of the big motor, for us to get out. I approached the truck and told him the other guy he passed at the gate said it was OK.

"NO! Get out. This is private. You can't fish here!" he ordered.

We saddled up and drove the trucks the 200 yards upstream to the public access the pickup driver had mentioned, which is what we were looking for in the first place, and parked next to the river again. Walking upstream for about 150 yards revealed a small break that dumped into the bottom of a slow side channel. It formed a perfect spot to fish and was big enough for both to drift without intruding on each other. The current tumbling off the break gave the water just enough texture to provide the fish with a measure of cover. They rose without trepidation. It also gave the dry fly just enough deceit to make it appear to be struggling—an irresistible sight for any rising trout. That is exactly what I tied on—the old reliable "Irresistible". We cast the fly above the break and let it cascade naturally into the run. Jack's first drift was perfect. Halfway through it, a wild Rainbow took his fly with authority. It broke water and was airborne several times before he managed to get it on the reel. The little break fished wonderfully, as did the braid into which it joined. Even the slack water below it was productive. I caught several fish while inadvertently grease lining the fly behind me as I moved a few steps upstream. Jack called me on that, every time.

"That's ungentlemanly Cahill. You're not supposed to cast downstream."

"I wasn't casting. I was just keeping the rod loaded while I moved up."

"It's still contrary to proper technique, "he insisted.

We had a magnificent dry fly evening until the pitch of night stopped us. Stumbling our way back to the trucks along the water's edge by the dots of our headlamps, Jack commented on our good fortune in being kicked out by the dump truck driver. I agreed. We had caught many fish in the short span of the gloaming. We drove the 5 miles up Anthracite Creek to the campground and selected a good site. It was after Labor Day and before hunting season, so the campground was empty. We had planned the trip specifically to avoid any crowds. It worked. We knew what we were doing, at least that time. I lit a Coleman lantern and set it on the picnic table while Jack made cocktails. We sat by the fire and imbibed. Jack broached the subject of our chicken stores. Again I assured that I had plenty in the cooler

Drinks finished, we moved to the picnic table to have our meal before relaxing by the fire and discussing the evenings catch. I pulled the chicken and salads from the cooler and set a civilized table. We each pulled a piece of chicken from the large bag on the table and began to eat. I was hungry. I'm sure he was because he had asked about the chicken at least three times since the DOT yard.

Seconds into chewing the first bite he looked at me. I could tell instantly that something wasn't right. Little beads of sweat dotted his brow. His mouth was agape and the look on his face so distressed that I thought he was having a stroke or a heart attack. Through his mouthful he said, "Is your chicken really spicy, Cahill? Is it HOT?"

That's what I was thinking, "This stuff is spicy!"

We turned our heads and expectorated the mouthful simultaneously. He took another piece form the bag and sniffed it. I did the same.

Tentatively, we took a nibble—same thing. We went through every piece in the bag. It was all super spicy, unbearably hot and inconsumable, So much for dinner.

"Where did you get this chicken?" he asked.

"Same as you, the Super Market Deli," I replied holding up the bag.

"Did a Mexican give it to you?"

"Well, yes," I said.

"Next time you get us chicken, Cahill, make sure a . . . ." I cut him off in mid sentence.

"Stop right there. I am not going to say—no-no-no, I want a white guy to give me my chicken. Have you lost your mind?" I admonished.

"Well, I'm hungry!" he said through a mouth full of lettuce and dressing.

We laughed out loud at the ludicrous suggestion and ate our salads by the light of the Coleman lantern, in the chill of a fine September evening. I couldn't believe that he didn't have some of those freeze-dried meals. I asked him. He didn't. I did, at home in my camping stores.

After dinner, (salads & cookies), we had another cocktail while we sat by the fire. As we relaxed in the deafening silence of a fireside trance, the switch flipped and the light came on.

"Oh, my God!" I proclaimed, struck by revelation.

"What?" he said with a Vodka tongue.

"That's why the dump truck guy kicked us out."

"What?" with the same tongue.

"I gave the first guy a piece of chicken—right? A piece of my chicken—not your chicken that we were eating when he drove up—we were eating the last of that."

"Yeah, so?" He still didn't get it.

"He ate the chicken while he was driving out. I saw him take a bite as he pulled away. It burned the hell out of his mouth, just like it did to us. When he turned onto the highway the dump truck was just coming through the gate. I saw it. He radioed the dump truck driver to kick us out. All those trucks have radios. He thought we were messing with him," I explained.

"I'll be damned," he said. "I think you're right."

"I know I'm right."

"I'm glad you gave that guy a piece," he allowed.

As I sat there in my lawn chair, head back, feeling fat and happy, a shooting star or satellite passed overhead, creasing the night sky. I watched it travel a long way before it made a sharp right turn and continued out of sight behind the ridge.

"That was weird," I thought.

I sat in silence, not wanting to say anything. I thought for a minute. Maybe it was two satellites crossing paths, or a couple of aircraft. The night sky can be deceiving; so can the cocktails. I really didn't want to say anything.

"What the hell was that—Cahill?" Jack asked.

"Oh crap, he saw it too," I thought.

"I don't know—UFO maybe." Jack downed his cocktail and stood from the lawn chair.

"I'm going to bed before I get a painful physical examination," he announced.

With that said, he crawled into the back of his pickup, as if the aluminum camper shell and can of bear mace I knew he kept in it would foil an alien abduction.

I haven't taken chicken to eat on a fishing trip since then. I had a similar experience with a bottle of soy sauce—can't go near the stuff now.

# Drift 3

# Ssss

Wildlife always plays a role in the act of fishing, especially for fly fishermen. They tend to gravitate towards secluded, if not remote, spots to ply their skills. It is my contention that for those of us who seek the more remote locations those encounters with wildlife are far more frequent, often entertaining, and occasionally flat out dangerous. The primary species in such encounters is of course the fish, but deer, elk, bighorns, raptors, fowl, rodents, snakes, moles and voles are always about. They provide an interesting backdrop to the main event, if one cares to look up from the fly or the water.

As a kid fishing with Jack in Utah, I was constantly on the lookout for snakes, rattlers to be exact. They still scare the pants off me. They are ubiquitous along the mountain creeks of the Uintah and Wasatch Mountains. I often froze in my tracks upon my youthful encounters with them. When I discovered there are no rattlers in the central Rockies around Aspen, a great burden was lifted from my fishing experience. I think it may be one of the factors that has kept me close to those waters for over 35 years. This is not to say I have not encountered snakes or rattlers during that time. I just have not seen the latter on what I consider my home water.

Some years ago, Jack and I planned a trip to the Miracle Mile on the North Platte in Wyoming. I had never fished the legendary stretch between the two reservoirs, Seminole and Pathfinder, and looked forward to the trip as much as any I have taken.

We left on Memorial Day, figuring the campgrounds and river would be empty after the holiday weekend. We found the place deserted and set up camp at a site below the upper reservoir's dam. It was a good site just off the river bank, well timbered with big ponderosas.

It was hot the first afternoon and the fishing was slow. We kept trying different runs and pools, working our way up and down the river. If you don't catch a fish, only two choices are available: change the fly or move. We did both all afternoon without success. After frothing all the water reachable on foot around our camp site we were at our wits' end. As often is the case, the legendary river was not living up to its legend. Above our camp, the walls between which the dam is secured rise like sentinels from the river bed. We decided on a little rock climbing to reach the tail-race of the dam, which is basically inaccessible, blocked by the large boulders and scree that have, over the eons, tumbled to the river from the walls above. Beyond the obstruction was good, fishable water and we were sure that not many took the trouble to attempt the hardscrabble climb to fish it. We set off late that afternoon along the sunbaked rubble. The climb was torturous in neoprene waders, vest and packs. But we continued undaunted. About halfway to our reward, we leaned against the shady side of a big boulder to cool ourselves and replenish our fluids.

"You think there are any snakes around here?" Jack asked while looking intently at the rest of our course. I knew what he meant. He had the same thought I did while trudging through the stone monoliths. It was typical rattler country.

"No, the elevation here is too high. I checked the altimeter at camp and it's about the same as Aspen," I told him, reassuring myself as well.

Finally the route became impassable and we had to turn back. With ample light left in the day we decided to give the river another try around the camp. After all, we'd come to fish. The hike back down was equally exhausting, and I was glad to reach the ease of foot the river trail provided.

Directly in front of our camp the trail forked. The right fork went to a large pool protected by a big boulder and the left circumvented it and curved back to the water's edge. Jack went left and I headed for the big boulder and pool. As we split our course the ominous sound of a rattler scared us. I stopped dead in my tracks as taught so many years before, and looked for the source of the sound. Jack did the same on his side of the fork.

There, between the two forks, coiled and vibrating like an alarm clock, was the biggest rattler I've ever seen, outside of a zoo or some exhibit of stuffed critters. It looked to be five feet long even in its coiled posture. The head was as big as a hamburger bun and it was exactly the color of the rocks we had just extracted ourselves from upriver. It was, in a word, unnerving. I took a few steps back and made a wide swing around it, following Jack down the left fork.

"I thought you said there weren't any snakes around here?" He castigated.

I had no response. What could I say? It's what I'd thought. Suddenly, I was back in my youth. That old feeling crept its way up my spine resulting in a cold shiver at the nape of my neck. As we walked down the trail I followed him, sweeping the ground and underbrush with my rod tip. I poked that thing under every bush and rock along that river during the remains of the day. When we came back upstream toward camp we approached the trail's fork cautiously. The snake was gone. This was even more frightening. With camp only a few yards away, I began to fret over its' location. At night I poked under my tent and sleeping bag with my rod. In fact, I couldn't even go to the outhouse without it or some other long stick in my hand. For the next three days I poked every conceivable snake hiding place along that river, to the point of worry about wearing the tip feral off my rod. I was never comfortable in that campsite. It was the biggest snake I'd ever encountered in the wild, and the scariest. I didn't see another snake while fishing the North Platte.

Of course, there are plenty of harmless western garden snakes in the mountains around my home waters. I see them frequently. Yet I was surprised by a snake encounter on the fabled Gunnison River, a mile or two above its confluence with the North Fork at a spot we call the "Sucker Hole".

It is a long, deep, placid section, that when fished below the surface can yield some of the biggest suckers around. I know a Sucker on a fly rod sounds sacrilegious, but It happens. There the river is wide, flat and deep. One side has a shallow gravel bar that slopes into the main current and presents an impossible drift. The deep holding water is just too far away and despite the longest cast one can make, the swifter shallow water puts a large bow in the line, resulting in a rip of the fly and a relatively shallow drift. The other side is flanked by the trail and a sharp, grassy bank. Depending on the river's flow, the water can be right at grass level. The deep run looks inviting. I can rarely resist fishing it as I make my way up or down stream to the more productive waters at either end. However, the current speed is deceiving and it is difficult to get a fly down to where the fish are holding. When I do manage to reach the bottom, I usually get hung up and end the drift by snapping off my rig. I hardly ever catch anything but suckers there, if I remember to put six or eight split shot above my double rig of egg pattern and some other wet fly. I don't really expect to catch anything in that run, but I always work it at a cast and step pace from the grassy bank, as a matter of paying dues I suppose.

After a long day's march from the North Fork access to the Smith Fork some three or four miles up the gorge, Jack and I stopped for a rest and perfunctory fish at the Sucker Hole on our way back to the truck. We were just about to stand and give the run our dues paying drift when I noticed a Garden snake emerge from a clump of buffalo grass on the bank directly in front of us. I pointed out the snake for Jack.

It slithered to the water's edge and stuck its head over the smooth black current. We sat still, allowing it to proceed. Instead it tapped the water with the underside of its jaw in a series of little pecks, just barely breaking the skim. It did this several times over the course of a few minutes. Each time it held a statue's pose, head extended over the water.

"What the hell is that snake doing Cahill?" Jack asked equally mystified by the creature's behavior.

"I think it's getting a drink." I gave the only answer I could conjure; I thought it was getting a drink. I had never seen a snake drink. But it didn't drink.

We stood cautiously to get a better look. It was only five or six feet in front of us. The snake tapped the water again and froze with its head a hair off the surface. Seconds passed. A small trout fry came up to investigate and the snake grabbed it with the speed only a wild thing possesses. With the little fish firmly gripped, it slithered back to the buffalo grass hideaway and began the process of swallowing it. It was fishing, not drinking. I didn't know snakes could fish. But they do. And they do it the same way dry fly fisherman do, by tricking the fish to the surface.

The snake was imitating the surface disturbance created by a large bug or terrestrial creature, such as a mouse or frog. He tricked that little trout and it paid the ultimate price. The snake was not a catch and release fisherman. I am still amazed at what you can see if you just stop and look.

I have a whole new respect for snakes since, but I still don't like them.

Looking up the Gunnison River Gorge where the snake caught the fish

# Drift 4

# For the Birds

As I think back on all the days I have spent holding a fly rod, I occurs to me that a great deal of time has been spent observing or interacting with wildlife. It just happens if you spend enough time in the wilds. Often comical, sometimes amazing, and occasionally dangerous, wildlife is an integral part of the fishing experience. The fish, of course, are wildlife but they are also the prey. When some dangerous creature that can kill, eat or at least damage you is encountered, you get the sense of what it means to be prey. Granted the fish are tricked into becoming prey, even though they live under the constant threat of death from above. We humans who invade the domains of those larger creatures that can consume us are not tricked into that position, only enticed by our atavistic desires to hunt, fish, or gather. It has given me a respect for the creatures that share this earth with us; the fish are not the least of those. Maybe it's why I practice catch and release. They are among the few creatures of such a wild nature that can actually be handled by us, with minimal risk to either party, without a weapon and in most cases without the aid of machinery. It's damn hard, if not impossible, to catch a large ungulate, bruin, or canine without the aid of a net, let alone handle it and take a good look at its magnificence.

Yet I have had the distinct luck and pleasure to do just that on many occasions: take a good look, that is. I have never openly sought such encounters. They simply seem to happen as a side bar of proximity. Such doesn't occur while riding in the truck or watching TV. One has to place himself where the action is in order to observe it firsthand. By doing so I have been delighted, astounded, and flat scared shitless.

Normally, birds of any kind would not be considered a dangerous species. When was the last time you heard about someone being accosted by a bird? Oh sure, I've had hummingbirds dive bomb me while I was wearing something red, and nesting starlings have taken a swoop at my hair when I've passed too close to their nest. Generally, all one must do to stop the encounter is to wave a hand or a hat, and that's that. Knowing that is of little comfort when an obstreperous avian sets its sights on you.

Jack and I were getting ready for an afternoon fish at the old Forest Service tree farm access on the Roaring Fork in El Jebel one frosty spring day. I sat on the icy tailgate of my pickup, peeling off my street clothes to don long johns and waders. My ass was cold blue. I rushed like hell to get dressed and beat Jack to the ready by a few steps at least. It is a rare occasion, indeed, that my poor abused bottom is not either frozen or fried while getting into fishing togs. That tailgate can heat up like a griddle in only a minute when dropped into the sun. This day, however, the sun had no effect on it because there wasn't any. It was one of those in-between season kind of days—almost full spring but cold enough that metal can put a chill to the bone when bare skin is applied to it for a few seconds. I really don't know which is worse, a roasted butt or a frozen one. Dressed and ready, I tossed the truck keys to Jack.

"Lock up when you get done, will you? I'll see you down on the river."

"Hold a minute. I'm almost ready," he begged.

"I'll walk slowly. Just hurry up. You rig like an old lady," I carped. "Make sure you lock up that camper shell."

"Hey! How about you kiss my ass?" he parried.

"Only if you draw a circle around it so I can tell it from your face and warm it up a little. Come on."

I walked the dozen or so yards to the green metal gate that designates the access point through the property. The Forest Service sign on the post next to it instructs the user to "Please Close the Gate". Jack fussed with the camper shell lock and cursed the wrong key.

For some reason, I opened the gate with the hand holding my fly rod. I guess my other hand was full of pack. When I stepped through, I shut the gate as instructed, again with my hand holding the fly rod straight up into the air. I shoved it forward hard, a little distempered by my cold ass and Jack's dawdling. When the gate snapped to, my fly rod twanged and nearly came loose from my grip. I heard an audible thwack and cringed, thinking I had slammed the tip against an overhanging tree limb, and mentally chastised myself for damaging the rod in my haste. I looked up to check the tip, concerned that I may have broken it. Then from behind me, I heard the screech of a raptor. When I turned to look, a bird fell out of the sky hitting the ground only 15 or 20 feet past the gate. Next, a hawk landed in a Gambel Oak grove another ten feet beyond. It raised hell, flapping its wings in protest, punctuated by a few more angry screeches.

"Jesus! Did you see that?" Jack exclaimed.

"No, but I felt it. Did what I think, just happen?"

"That was unbelievable. When you shut the gate your fly rod tip knocked that bird from the hawk's talons. I think you hit the hawk square in the chest."

Its prey, a small red house finch, twitched on the ground. I was a little afraid to continue down the trail, as I would be between the Finch and the angry Raptor. I could see the headlines: "Fisherman blinded by mad hawk!" I waited at the gate for Jack to catch up. We passed the downed bird cautiously and together, hoping the combined mass of our bodies would dissuade the angry hawk from any vengeful act. I sure didn't want it thinking I was going to take its meal. Thankfully, we made it past the scene without incident, the hawk still screeching complaints in the background. Some yards down the trail, I turned back to see the little finch regain its senses and fly into the Gambel Oaks protection. They say timing is everything in life. I'll let the hawk and the finch attest to that. Can I have a witness, brothers and sisters?

Now, one would think that a beautiful waterfowl like a Goose couldn't represent a threat to a fisherman. But I'm here to tell you that Geese in general are mean. I used to work for a man in Aspen who was a bird freak. He kept all manner of exotic birds on his property. There were Guinea Fowl, Golden Pheasants, Lady Amherst, Blue Eared Manchurian Pheasants, Toulouse Geese, Red and Blue Macaws and household birds, like Parakeets and Cockatiels. He also had a number of wild but resident lesser Canada Geese and a pair of Black Swans. He even kept a special pair of endangered Trumpeter Swans that were given to his care after the filming of a wildlife special with a famous entertainer. They released the Swans for the cameras on the upper Roaring Fork River, which bisected his property. Of course the Swans were recaptured immediately after the filming, for such a valuable breeding pair of endangered creatures could not be left to roam the second home-riddled section of the river. I was there that day, building a new barn on the property. We had to stop work because the filmmakers were trying to simulate wilderness and could not afford the sound of power saws, hammers and cursing carpenters on the sound track, and because all the racket would spook the Swans. Because I was there, they called for me to help round up those huge birds, and I found out the hard way that they pack a punch. When those things draw their neck back and throw their beaked head forward like an Ali jab, you know you've been hit. I was building a rock wall in the same man's yard when his Black Swans got loose and punched my hamstrings in the same manner, while I was occupied shoveling cement. The blows brought me to my knees. I had to fend them off with my shovel while I made a getaway to safer ground. The bruises lasted for quite some time.

So during the spring nesting season I am always wary of the many Canada Geese that take up residence on the little grassy islands and shores of most western rivers. The lower Roaring Fork is no exception. Even my seventy-pound Weimaraner bitch takes flight when she encounters them on the river. You would think a bird dog of such renown and breeding would give chase. The fact is she'll chase chickens, ducks, pheasant and doves but when she sees a Canada Goose her cowardice shines through. I can't get her off my leg and sometimes she'll obstinately wait downstream of them, no matter how vigorously I cajole her to pass while fishing my way up river. Clearly there is no bigger coward than a dog outside its own yard.

So when Jack and I fished the lower Roaring Fork at Catherine's Store one early April day, I was on my guard. The Geese were everywhere on that section of river. We had a wonderful day catching and releasing fish. We were about two miles upstream from the truck. The Denver Western & Rio Grande tracks run along the river all the way to Aspen, with the right of way being the only means of access along that stretch.

Tired, hungry, and ready for the day's-end beer, we decided to mount the steep bank from the river bottom to the tracks above, making our walk a little easier. But believe me, old unused railroad bed is not the easiest surface to walk along. The ties aren't spaced for a person's normal stride, and the coke ballast around them is always at some obtuse angle that makes walking in waders and boots difficult and tiring at best. Still, it was an easier path than the cobbled river bed or its sharply angled, brush covered bank. The latter is mostly impassable in that section anyway. The flat side of the river is private property, so our choices were limited.

I let Jack take the lead and waited until he reached the top, for safety's sake. It's a basic rule of climbing. If he stumbled or slid I didn't want his 225 pound frame steamrolling me down. I stood watching his path in case such happened, that I might know where not to step when it was my turn. Almost to the top, he grunted a few times as the loose ground gave way and he scrambled to regain his footing. I was just about to holler "watch out," but before I could speak a dark shape passed over my head from the river behind me.

A big gander landed square on the nape of Jack's neck, hooking its feet into the collar of his vest. The bird started pecking the back of his head with its beak and beating him about the ears with the elbows of its wings. The sound of those wings cutting the air was horrific, and the bird honked and chattered. I actually started to laugh until I realized how distressed he was-Jack, not the bird.

I scrambled up the slope as fast as I could, but the felt soles of my wading boots provided about as much traction as a dog gets while executing a sharp turn on linoleum. I just couldn't make headway fast enough. Then a thought occurred to me. What the hell was I going to do with or to the big gander?"

While I spun my wheels, Jack screamed like a little girl being accosted by a big bumble bee.

"Cahill, get it off me!" he pleaded

I couldn't get up there, let alone get to the bird. At length, Jack managed to get his hat off and started fighting back by swatting it. Then I started to worry about my own predicament. Were there any more geese? Would the gander turn on me and attack me frontally?

Finally, Jack made contact to the thing's head with the metal adjusting clasp on the back of the hat. I heard a thwack and the big bird peeled off, gliding back to the river.

We walked the two miles back to the truck in utter fear of another attack. I think word had gone down the Goose grapevine, because several flew from the river to buzz us. At least by then we were onto them and could use our fly rods to fend them off, which we did. Now I have some empathy for my dog's feelings about the damn things. Geese are just flat mean.

Hawks and geese are one thing, but my encounter with a bald eagle on the Lake Fork of the Gunnison left me wary of them, as well.

Fall fishing can produce some of the best days anyone could hope for on many of our rivers. The tourists have gone for the season, and generally only the leaf lookers are about, who rarely get out of their vehicles. I don't know how they manage to see anything driving like they do. But at least they're not wandering around the river with their cameras and tripods spooking the fish. The kids are back in school, which means the campgrounds are mostly empty until hunting season, and we generally have the woods to ourselves. If the weather is still good enough to fish during hunting season I wear a blaze orange ball cap with the letters, "MAN" written in black magic marker across the fore crown. This might sound stupid, but over-amped hunters sitting on some ridge overlooking the river from half a mile distant have a way of shooting first and saying they're sorry later. Many a dead cow is evidence to that. I call cows—"slow elk."

Once, while belly boating at Seller Lake on the Hagerman Pass road, some hunters from New York asked me how old a deer has to get before it becomes an elk; no kidding. I got out of there fast. I haven't been shot yet so I guess the hat works. I've had an arrow or two whizz by during bow season.

It was mid-November and the weather was perfect. We hadn't seen the faintest hint of snow yet, and I talked Jack into driving from Carbondale to the Lake Fork for a last chance to fish before winter set in. This was not unusual for us. We have floated the Gunnison Gorge as late as the first week in December. I won't forget that day soon, because I fell in just below the Smith Fork and spent a very uncomfortable day working my way down the river while sitting on top of my belly boat.

This particular Saturday in November was unseasonably warm and sunny-shirt sleeve weather. We arrived at the Lake Fork of the Gunnison around 11 a.m. and started our day's fish, right above the Red Bridge campground. The river was very low and clear. At the time the entire state was in the middle of very bad drought. Snow pack levels were so low in some drainages, that spring runoff was barely noticeable. Hence, the fishing was difficult, but at least we were out and not home performing honey-dews or watching TV.

The Lake Fork has become quite a fishery over the last decade. And I love to fish it whenever I can, even though it takes some time to reach from just about anywhere in the state except Lake City, which it runs through. But the section that we were fishing was in fact water newly opened to the public on what was formerly a private ranch. Considerable time and money had been spent improving the river habitat with the addition of quite a number of wing dams. And beyond that, the DOW had kept the new section closed to the public for about four years after acquisition, while conducting habitat improvements and allowing the fish population to grow. It worked, and the river was a premier fishery until some rancher upstream spilled a storage tank of fuel oil in it. But that was after the day in question.

We worked the river very hard with little result. Yet the place is so beautiful, and the drive so long to get there, we couldn't bring ourselves to quit. After lunch we were rewarded by the sight of a bald eagle perched in the denuded limbs of an ancient cottonwood tree along the river. The bird was majestic. It's not often that I get to see one close up. Usually they are soaring or flying at such heights, they are only recognizable by the distinct white head. But this bird was less than 50 yards away and I could tell that it was watching us, as intently as we it. I couldn't take my eyes off it, and almost fell in several times while stupidly walking and watching. Finally, with my gaze still on the bird, I stumbled for the last time against the bottom of a large wing dam. I mounted it to continue up the river, but decided better to walk along its length and fish the large, deep holding pool it created. I could feel that eagle's stare as I stepped along the manmade jetty. Jack worked the water on the other side of the river, just even with my position, but not quite under the monolithic cottonwood perch from which the large avian surveyed us.

At the end of the wing dam, I peeled some line from my reel to make a long cast into the upper reaches of the inviting pool. When I looked down to make sure I had good footing on the end of the biggest rock, I saw a huge Brown Trout lying at the very end of the last flat boulder around which the current gleefully skirted. The fish was a good 24 inches in length. The rock was wet all around its contour; one eye and a gill were gone from it. It was a fresh catch. I called to Jack across the river.

"Can you see this from there?"

"What is it?"

"About a two-foot brown. It's still wet with the eye and a gill plucked. I think our friend in the tree is the owner."

When Jack started across the river below the wing dam to have a look, the eagle went nuts. It left the tree and made a low pass over us, screeching as it glided just feet over our heads. My knee-jerk reaction was to duck, even though it had already passed me. Jack stepped to the wing dam and inspected the fish. The eagle strafed us again. It was trying to run us off from the catch. The eerie screech put a chill in my bones.

"I get it. This is a fresh catch. I think the fish is so big that the eagle had trouble getting airborne with it and landed on this rock instead of flying away to that cottonwood or its nest. I'll bet we spooked it off the fish when we walked up. That's why it appeared so suddenly in that tree," Jack offered.

"Let's move up before it comes back," I cautioned.

We did, and about 200 yards upstream we came upon another brown trout of equal size in a shallow gravel bottom pool. It was making a redd.

"I'll bet that's the mate. Those big browns are up from the lake spawning," Jack calculated.

"Yeah, and I'm sure that's why the fishing is so slow, with that eagle flying up and down the river. Funny we didn't notice him earlier," I added.

We watched the big fish for an hour or so. It alternately flailed its tail against the gravel bottom and then swam around the shallow run. Obviously, it was looking for the other fish. It was a sad scene, but that's the way of nature. All is not fair in love and dinner.

Jack and I left the river for the road which runs parallel to it, hoping we could see the eagle dining on the big brown. But there was too much brush in the way to see the wing dam. I'm sure it was down there because it wasn't in the big cottonwood when we passed by.

That was worth the drive.

# Drift 5

# The Black Vole

I have an old and dear friend who once assisted a biologist in the study of Voles. Actually, the assistance amounted to a one day trip to collect specimens in the field, the object of which was to trap the lesser known and more rare Red Vole. The Black Vole is ubiquitous, but this biologist's thesis paper was on the Red Vole, and he needed live specimens to complete his work. My friend took it seriously and did a little research before the trip to familiarize himself with the habits and habitat of the Vole.

As he tells the story, they spent the day collecting the numerous traps set by the biologist. My friend would pull the traps from their location and call the catch to the biologist, who stood by with his log recording the information. Then the Vole was released and the trap relocated. The biologist would record the traps new location on a map. Time after time each trap yielded a black vole and not the sought red. Evidently this was important information, as it helped to establish the ratio of Blacks to Reds which was part of the study. However the biologist's disappointment was obvious to my friend, as the day wore on and no Red Voles were collected.

Eventually my friend, a dedicated prankster and humorist, decided to lighten the mood. He retrieved a trap and hid it from the biologist with his crouched body

"What's in that one?" the biologist inquired.

"Crap," my friend answered. "It's just another Goddamn *Clethronamise Gaperi*"—the scientific name for the Black Vole, a term the biologist had never uttered, but my friend had learned from his limited research.

He said the biologist cracked up and the mood of the disappointing field trip was greatly elevated. I always liked that story and filed it away for safekeeping.

Many years later, Jack and I were at Deep Lake in the Flat Tops Wilderness of the White River National Forest. Deep Lake is where the state record for Lake Trout was taken in the 1940's. It is also the site of a hotel that was an overnight stop on the old stage road from Glenwood Springs to Meeker. It is said that Teddy Roosevelt stayed there on one of his hunting trips. The hotel burned down long ago and only a sign at the lake gives the visitor any inkling of the area's history.

We arrived there late on a summer afternoon to fish the evening hatch from our belly boats. But the purpose of our trip was to fish the South Fork of the White River above the falls. The best fishing on the South Fork is above the falls. The river below is populated mostly by whitefish, which are not a trout fisherman's preferred species. The falls can be reached from the Meeker side of the Flat Tops, but not without a serious hike, which leaves little time in the day to fish. So, by approaching the South Fork from the Glenwood side we could ease our access and fish Deep Lake to boot. It was only a nine mile drive from Deep Lake to Budge's Resort on the South Fork—no hiking involved.

The evening fish at Deep Lake was productive, and we enjoyed a clear, star-filled night at the campsite with the mesmerizing flicker of a fire at our feet. The next morning dawned bright and clear. We fixed a hasty breakfast, broke camp, and loaded my faithful F-250 for the nine mile drive. Nine miles on a four-wheel-drive wilderness road takes a bit of time to cover so we made a slow enough pace to enjoy the scenery as we jostled our way to the river.

There's a public parking area for the South Fork trail adjacent to Budge's. The resort's corral is not far from it, and the flies that go along with all the trail riding horses made donning our gear a misery. We had to walk a good half-mile downstream before we were shed of them. Jack cursed the entire time. I have to admit the damn things were a nuisance.

Free of the troublesome flies, we began to fish and had a darn good morning. If you get far enough below Budge's, where the city slickers that frequent the lodge are too timid to venture, it turns into real wilderness fishing. We did alright that morning. The fish weren't that big but there wasn't a fly, a person or a whitefish in sight. It was a good morning. Of course, the trek had left us depleted. We had made almost three miles as we fished our way downstream. I could hear the roar of the falls in the distance.

Jack picked the lunch spot on the water's edge under a copse of evergreens. We made ourselves comfortable on the shady moss-covered bank, our feet resting in the sand and gravel below the cut bank. We talked about allowing the little river to settle down before we fished our way back to the truck. Of course that meant a nap. As I fussed with my pack and vest to make a pillow, Jack sat staring between his feet.

"Hey Cahill what's this?" he said pointing to a little rodent between his feet, resting on the sand and gravel below the moss-covered cut bank that was our seat.

I looked over the edge to his wading boots. There, sniffing the felt sole of his upturned boot toe, was a Black Vole. I couldn't believe my luck. I had waited years for this opportunity.

"*Cletheronamise Gaperi*," I said.

# Drift 6

# Pay your money and take your chances

In Alaska, bears are part of fishing. It is rare that one does not encounter them while fishing there, especially if doing so in the wilderness. However, I did spend a week in a Forest Service cabin at Church Cove on Gambier Bay, along the shore of Admiralty Island, without seeing any. But Jack, Sheets and I fished out of a motorized raft. We were on the water most of the day and did not return to camp until late each day. It was an unusual trip.

Our first day out in the raft, we hit a large submerged rock and promptly shattered the wooden strap-on transom which held our ten-horse outboard to the raft. Sheets held the outboard upright on the broken transom while Jack steered us in retreat from Gambier Bay. I stood in the bow of the raft, on lookout for any submerged obstructions which might cause further damage. It was all we could do to get back to the beach at Church Cove.

This represented a serious setback. The fish were not in the little creek that emptied into the recesses of Church Cove, and if we were to locate a run we needed the raft and motor to search the numerous drainages into Gambier Bay. On the beach, Jack and I quickly removed the outboard from the shattered transom, and then the transom from the raft. We got a better look at the damage once we had the thing free of the straps that secured it to our craft. The entire port gusset was shattered, useless. We couldn't row around Gambier Bay because the current and tides would surely take us out into the Frederick Sea. We had to fix it, but how?

As Jack and I sat on the porch of the little cabin contemplating our plight, I noticed a few lengths of bailing wire hanging from nails driven into the cabin wall. We decided the wire would work well for fastening a brace to the transom's shattered port gusset; but what to use for a brace? We tried every piece of firewood we could find. None of it had the shape or rigidity required to support a ten-horse outboard under the stress of operation. We sat for a while discussing our options. Then I noticed the camp bow saw leaning against the cabin wall. The steel frame was exactly the shape of the broken gusset. I removed the blade and held the frame against the broken transom. It was perfect. We used the bits of bailing wire to fasten it to the gusset. But it was still loose and we knew it would not suffice for use with the outboard. We found some 1' x 2' trim under the cabin porch and wired them into the transom frame to stiffen the whole mess. We needed more wire, but we had used all there was. I retrieved a rafting strap from a dry bag full of fishing gear, and wrapped it around the vertical 1 x 2 brace that supported the gusset leg. Satisfied with our ingenious repair, despite the limited resources, I turned the transom flat on the deck. Jack stood on it and gave several sharp bounces of his 180-pound frame. It held. We were back in business.

We quickly reattached the transom and outboard to test it in the less treacherous waters of Church Cove. It worked. The outboard was secure and did not wobble or vibrate the transom apart under operation. We motored the raft to the upper end of the cove, where Sheets was casting fruitlessly into the feeder creek for Salmon that weren't there. He had begged off from the repair efforts, claiming ineptitude at mechanical contrivances. We were thankful for it.

"Come on Sheets, quit that water frothing and get in. We're gonna' test this baby out," I yelled over the clatter of the outboard.

He approached tentatively, while Jack held the raft still in the current with a little throttle applied to the motor. He didn't get in, but instead turned a skeptical eye to the repaired transom on the stern.

"I don't know. Maybe I'll just stay here. That thing looks a little Rube Goldbergy to me," he complained.

"Just get in. There are no fish here. You're flicking at empty water," I pointed out.

"OK, but if that thing breaks, I'm not rowing. You guys fixed it—you can row." He was emphatic, as he threw a leg over the gunwale.

We slowly putted around the waters of Church Cove and the adjacent shoreline of Gambier Bay that day and the next. Neither Jack nor I cared to row, so we didn't get too far from the cabin at first. Finally gaining enough confidence that our repaired transom was seaworthy and not likely to fail, we ventured fully out into Gambier Bay. We had seen numerous seals hunting salmon in the full salt of the bay. As no sign of our prey was to be found in the little streams and creeks, we felt sure the fish were holding in the bay proper. We followed the seals and anchored the raft in the midst of what appeared to be their hunting ground.

We were, of course, outfitted as fly fishermen, for we fully intended to use our skill as such on the creeks in the area. But as those creeks were void of fish, the open water of the bay was the only option we had left, and fly rods are not the best tool under such conditions. Nonetheless, we wore our arms out casting big 8 & 10 weight rods from the raft. We used lead core leaders and lots of split shot to get the fly down into the current. It was difficult fishing at best. What else could we do but this, or sit in the cabin and while away the days until the plane came to pick us up. Spending the day in the raft was the better choice, since at least we were able to see the country and wildlife in the area.

As we strip jerked our flies through the dark waters of Gambier Bay, seals rose constantly around us. They are curious creatures by nature, and our presence intrigued them to the point that they kept the fish either away or far too deep for us to reach. This wasn't working. We decided to try the seam water where Church Cove and the bay mingled. Perhaps the difference in current and temperatures would be a factor. Almost immediately, I was on. The thing actually surprised me. When the fishing is slow and almost pointless I am easily distracted by my surroundings, especially so in such magnificent country. There were seals to watch, eagles everywhere, and occasionally deer would show themselves on the shoreline, not to mention the seemingly limitless quantities of waterfowl. Hence, in my excitement at a striking fish I neglected to set the hook a second time, which is paramount with any Salmon. The hook does not sink well into the bony structure of their jaw, and that second set is necessary if the fish is to be landed.

The fish ran with the large Green Dace on the end of my line. Despite the drag set to full and my hand on the palming rim, I couldn't stop it. It breached several times, revealing itself to be a large King Salmon. On the last flight over the water the hook released, sending it back toward my head. I ducked and it missed. I cursed my luck, when I should have been cursing my failure to reset the hook. It was an exciting thirty seconds and gave us hope. I felt good, being one up on them with the only honest fish hooked yet. They jumped on the water where I caught the King, with a vengeance. I was forced to turn and fish the other side of the raft. Jack put on some extra weight to get the fly down, as I had done. He hooked up fairly soon after adjusting his depth. His big 10 weight rod bent to a visually uncomfortable arc. I feared for the rod's life. It stayed bent and twitched a few times. Jack stabbed the rods' fighting butt into his hip, hoping to gain some power on the fish.

"What the hell have you got on there, Jack? Sheets asked.

"I don't know, but whatever it is, Cahill and I are eatin' it."

He grunted while putting a big stroke on the rod, raising the fish the length of it. That's when the fish realized it was hooked. It took off and nearly drew Jack out of the raft. The line snapped and the rod twanged. Jack fell back on his ass, rod in hand and feet in the air.

The next day we ventured south to the next drainage at a place called Snug Cove, maybe six or eight miles from the cabin. We found the same picture there. And although the creek was open and quite fishable, it too was choked with hundreds of spawned-out pinks. They are not really worth the effort.

We decided to cross the open water of the bay to a little island that protruded from the salt like a Mohawk haircut atop an otherwise bald head. It seemed a likely spot from where to survey the open water of the bay, and we could see a small cozy beach on the side facing Snug Cove. The map calls it Gem Island. It is. The trip took about an hour. Motoring around the placid waters of little coves and shorelines is one thing, but the open water of the bay had a little chop and the raft a lot of drag. The trip was much like pushing a garden hose up a sand dune. We beached the raft and broke out the lunch supplies. There were many eagles in the trees along the shore, and we thought this was a good sign. Eagles don't usually hang out where the fish aren't.

As we sat on the beach enjoying lunch, I brought my binoculars to my eyes, checking the water for breaching Salmon. We had seen a lot of this, but despite their aerials I had hooked the only Salmon we had actually seen over the last three days. Just as I focused on the water a hundred yards off the beach, a large bull Seal breached to his midsection. Standing upright in the water, he clenched a huge Salmon in his teeth. I was awestruck by the sight of the fish wiggling in its jaws. Then with one twist of its massive head and neck it tossed the salmon some 40 or 50 feet through the air. The fish hit the water, emitting a distinctly audible splash. When it struck the surface, the Seal was there and came up from underneath to grab it again. I clearly saw the fish rise out of the water in the seal's mouth.

"Did you see that?" I hollered with the glasses still on my face.

They ignored me, while I kept the glasses on the water.

I lowered the binoculars when I didn't get a response. Sheets was running for the raft and Jack sat ready at the helm, jerking on the outboard's rip cord. I grabbed my lunch and ran to join them. Three guys never got back on the water so fast. As we raced at full speed for the seam water, where the action had taken place, Sheets yelled over the drone of the outboard for an explanation of what we had just witnessed.

"What the hell was that all about?" he demanded

"I'm not sure, but that was one big ass Salmon," I yelled back. From the stern Jack put in his two cents.

"He was trying to stun it. The fish was too big for him to handle."

It made sense to me. Jack cut the outboard and we drifted into the seam water—but nothing, no sign of the Seal or any other fish. We sat for some time in silence, rods in hand at the ready. I made a few fruitless cast-and-strip retrieves after counting the fly down at two feet per second. A Seal breeched behind us and barked a taunt.

After that, the weather turned and made venturing onto the bay even more treacherous. We continued to check the creeks in our area, making daily trips to the end of Church and Snug Coves looking for any signs that the Coho's were beginning to run. It was not to be. The fishing was poor and the weather as foul as it gets in southeast Alaska. It finally broke to a sunny day on the morning we were due to fly out.

But all was not a loss, for we had seen country that few are privileged to know, and the episode with the bull Seal was something I shall never forget. Jack and Sheets still talk about it when we recount our exploits. We had not seen a bear the entire stay.

That last morning was spent breaking camp, packing gear and stowing the raft and outboard in their containers. We piled it all on the beach and waited in our waders for the aircraft to arrive. In the distance, we could hear that unmistakable drone—the pilot was on time. However, it was not the DeHaviland Beaver which had delivered us, but rather a much larger twin engine Beech Craft. As we waded out to it with the gear, the pilot called out

"See any bears?" We told him no.

"We'll see what we can do about that on the way back." he said.

He was good to his word. He flew that big aircraft just feet off the deck up one of the larger rivers on Admiralty Island, wing tips way too close to the trees for me at 160 miles per hour. We saw bears.

Gem Island, Gambier Bay Alaska

Alaskan fresh water collection system

Rube Goldberg's transom repair

# Drift 7

# Gabby's Dilemma

Sometimes when I stand before the fly bins in a fly shop, I am stupefied by the selections. Considering the mayfly, caddis and stonefly are the three primary classes of insects in just about all Western rivers, it seems overkill that one could spend a small fortune stocking his fly box, or spend all his time trying to duplicate patterns available for sale commercially. The seemingly limitless variations lend an air of necessity to the angler. Surely any serious fly fisher would need at least three of each. Why else would they be available? I've seen anglers leave a fly shop with two hundred dollars worth of flies.

I realize that not every fly angler has the desire, ability or time to tie his own flies, but for me there is no other way to fish. Ever since Pip made that lure in the dirt-floor basement of the little house on Division St., I have felt the urge to twist my own. Granted, it took many years before I acquired the necessary tools and time to teach myself, but the effort required now seems paltry and distant. Oh, I purchase flies, but on a very limited basis. Mostly they are dry flies because they take so much time to tie, and because I use them for such a small window of the fishing year. For the most part I fish with what I tie. And so does Jack—fish with what I tie that is.

So it came as no surprise to me that I spent several weeks before a scheduled trip to Alaska's Anchor River tying salmon patterns. I put together one of those big flat Plano boxes of standards like Popsicles, Alaska Maryanne and Egg Sucking Leaches. It would turn out that my efforts, although commendable, were pointless.

After setting up camp with the RV along the spit that separates the Anchor from the salt of the Cook Inlet, we made our way to the first freshwater holding area some five or six hundred yards from the river's mouth. We called it the "Honey Hole", simply because the fish held there on their way upstream and were plentiful. In addition, the hole was big enough for a number of people to fish at the same time.

Jack, Joufisch and I were fishing it when Spoons joined us about mid morning. As Spoons began to pull line from his rod to make a first cast, the rod tip snapped in two. He was livid. He had already lost one rod to airline baggage handlers, which he'd discovered earlier that morning. Joufisch laughed a little too enjoyably, and it irritated Spoons even more.

"Damn, I feel like I've been violated by John Wayne with Gabby Hayes watching," he complained.

"Pull his britches aside, John. I can't see a damn thing," Joufisch quipped in a wonderfully accurate Gabby Hayes impression.

Luckily or wisely he'd brought three rods. He marched double-time up the spit for the RV. When he returned from the mile round-trip jaunt, it seemed that only a few casts had passed. He made good time, considering the waders and boots he wore and the loose sand that was the spit, but he was huffing for air.

I heard gasping as he approached, and turned my head to see him standing on the low sand rise about twenty feet behind me as he fiddled with a large rod and reel. I had to laugh and asked, "What the hell have you got, Spoons?"

"It's a 12 weight 15 foot Spay rod." The rod was enormous and the reel the diameter of a soup bowl.

"Good Christ! That thing is made for fishing fiords. How the hell are you going to use that here? I don't want any figure eights in the air over my head," I complained, referring to how the giant rod is used.

The caster draws a figure eight in the air with the rod tip. It takes a two-handed cast with ample slack line laid at the feet. The damn thing is made for big walled waterways—like a fiord. It is truly the artillery piece of fly casting.

"I'll just stand back here and flick it. Don't worry. I won't make any figure eights and I'll just catch bigger fish," he assured us, punctuating his remark with a slightly caustic tone.

"Spread out a little," Spoons commanded.

We did, hoping to humor him out of his grump. Jack and Joufisch opened the gap on either side of me, leaving a good fifty feet between each of us standing on the edge of the water. Spoons took a few more steps back away from the river and began to cast and drift the water above and below the three of us. We fished inside his reach. If the dots were connected, we formed a big triangle, a fishing phalanx if you will.

We covered a huge block of water and the phalanx allowed us to move up and down the river at will. It was beautifully constructed. Even our new-found symmetry didn't aid us. We did not catch fish. Nor did any of the dozen or so other anglers in the Honey Hole and along the river to the State Park entry. It was slow. The fish were there but it was slow.

At lunch we had a confab about what to do. We loved the camping spot. The silvers were in the river and we didn't want to leave. We had tried everything I'd tied in the previous weeks of preparation, but the fish just didn't show any interest. It is a fact that spawning Salmon do not strike at a fly out of hunger but rather out of territorial defense. The rhyme and reason of the strike can be baffling. They will strike at one fly but not another; it maybe the size, shape or color. Determining a fly that will trigger a strike is often a matter of trial and error; a hit a miss proposition that can go on all day until one has exhausted the contents of a fly box and even a whole vest. Sometimes they will take anything and sometimes they will take only one thing. So that is where we sat elbows on the RV kitchen table, chins resting in our hands; starring at a big pile of fuzz, feathers, tinsel and wire. After a bit, they decided that I should tie something large, green, yellow and orange—something garish. I struggled for a bit, attempting different configurations of that recipe, but none of my samples seemed to satisfy myself or the others. I held one up for all to see around the lunch table in the RV.

"That's stupid-looking!" Spoons spat out, still wallowing in the funk of his rod luck.

Finally I resorted to what I knew, and that was the standard trout fly configuration which I have tied so many times. After several more aborted attempts, I eventually contrived a large Pheasant Tail pattern on a number 2 hook. It contained all of the required criteria—big, green, yellow and orange-garish.

"This looks good, but we gotta' name it," Jack said.

All were silent and deep in thought, trying to conceive an appropriate name for the gaudy creation.

"Gabby's Dilemma," Jack insisted referring to Spoons' statement at the rod snapping.

We all agreed and shortened the moniker to "Gabby". The name stuck. We took the new fly to the Honey Hole and began to ply the waters. We formed the "Spoons Phalanx". On the first cast I was onto a large male Silver. Each of the others in turn garnered the same result. The other anglers in the general area of the Honey Hole were aghast at our seemingly expert prowess, and almost to a man sauntered by to watch us in action and inquire of our bait.

"What are you guys using?"

"A Gabby." They weren't sure if I was joshing them or not.

"A what?"

"It's just a pattern we thought up."

"Oh," was the usual response.

We caught and released silvers for the rest of the afternoon until our arms were cramped from the joy of such fishing. We physically could fish no more, and were beyond sated from our good luck. That afternoon we became the "Kings of the Spit".

That night I tied Gabbies until my eyes watered and we had enough for the rest of our stay on the Anchor. We fished up and down it for the next six days using the Gabby and getting the same result. One day a young fellow in his early teens showed up on the far side of the Honey Hole where a county road ended at the water's edge. I think it was a boat put-in, access to the Cook Inlet. He fished and watched us. Then while Jack hooked and fought another large Silver, the kid broached the subject of our bait.

"Did you catch that one on a Gabby?" he yelled across the water.

Jack and I looked at each other dumbfounded. The kid knew. Later that day another fly angler came by the Honey Hole and proclaimed he had been doing rather well in hooking and landing silvers. Always interested, I asked what he was using.

"I don't know," he said. "I found this thing down the way by the water's edge and thought I'd give it a try. Nothing else was working."

He unhooked a big fly from the keeper above his rod handle and held it in the palm of his hand for us to see. It was a Gabby that one of us had dropped on the sand shore at the river's mouth. I kept my mouth still and didn't divulge it to be one of my creations. I sure didn't want him to ask me for any. Even if I said no, which would be impolite and contrary to all the rules of fishing etiquette, he might offer to buy some. That is often the case with fly anglers who don't have what THEY think is the right fly. I can't say how many times I have heard, "Can I buy some of those off you?" while landing fish after fish in front of some poor guy that doesn't seem to have what he thinks he needs, which is rarely the fly I'm catching them on. We were trying to keep the source of the Gabby a secret, or else be placed under a siege of requests from anglers who fared less well. We didn't even show one to, Stan Harrington, the owner of Anchor Anglers, who had become our buddy over the last several visits to the area.

Alas, our time on the Anchor came to an end. Reluctantly we packed up the RV and drove the length of the spit back to the main road. We made a quick stop at Anchor Anglers to bid Stan farewell, thank him for all his courtesy, and to leave the last of our dry goods in the hope that he could distribute them to some needy souls along the river. We also wanted to leave a cooler with him that none could take back on their flights home.

As I walked into the fly shop with Jack, Spoons and Joufisch in close order behind me, Stan sat at his counter, furiously wrapping materials on a hook held fast in his fly tying vise.

"Rooster Cogburn and Company," he greeted.

"Stan, I see you're on duty today," I responded.

"God damn it, Rooster! I haven't left this vise in 3 days. Everybody on the river has been screaming for these Gabbies since you people got here."

It sounded more like Gabby's Revenge to me.

Gabby's Dilema

# Drift 8

# Rocky and Bullwinkle

Alaska's Kenai Peninsula is speckled with rivers and lakes, and is one of only a few places that can be fished from a vehicle. No fly-in is required to reach the famous Anchor River just 20 or so miles north of Homer. I met Jack and Earwig at the Anchorage airport about 12 A.M. in mid-August. We took a cab to the RV rental agency and spent the night in its parking lot. The privilege was afforded us by the RV agent, as our flight arrived so late. It is called "Bumpering In". They left us an RV door key in a hide-a-key box under the wheel well, sans ignition keys. To obtain those, we had to check in and pay the fee when the staff arrived in the morning. It's a very cool idea for late arrivers. The lot's proximity to a strip joint of some repute made for a late night—apparently it never closes. At least it seemed so that night. Jack and Earwig could not resist. I didn't go. Those places make me uncomfortable. I think they came back about 3 or 4 A.M. They were hard to wake in the morning and I had to conduct the check-in without them. In fact they didn't stir until I started the engine and began to pull away for our trip to the Anchor River some 4 hours south.

The middle of August had proved perfect for the arrival of Silver Salmon on a previous trip to the Anchor. We fished the first afternoon during the incoming tide at the river's mouth but failed to sight, let alone hook, any fish. This time the fish were a bit late. With the fishing slow, we made our way to the state park entry, where our old friend Stan Harrington operates Anchor Anglers just yards off the river. Stan was glad to see us, for it had been three years since we last fished there.

"Well, Rooster Cogburn and company!"

He greeted us referring to the old battered and floppy Stetson I so often wore while fishing. It's my Alaska hat. The thing has so much head grease that it holds water like a bowl. It's a great hat.

"You boys here for Silvers or Moose? If Moose, the season doesn't open until tomorrow and the Silvers are a little late."

"Silvers," I said. "We just came from the mouth but nothing was happening. Say, Stan, do you have a cooler we can borrow?"

"I still have the one you left here three years ago," he allowed and went to retrieve it from his shed.

We thanked Stan for the cooler and set out for the short drive to the campsite. That night we pulled our RV into the state park campground along the river, just downstream of Stan's shop. It's a great site, with the river only yards from the picnic table and fire pit. After a sumptuous meal of sockeye, which I had caught the previous day (again the only fish caught) while floating the upper Kenai River, we settled in around the fire to enjoy cigars and a fine old Port. Several glasses of Port into the old fireside trance, it was broken by a splashing in the river. I strained to peer through the black curtain draping the boundary of the fire's light and squinted to sharpen the Port haze. Two Moose sauntered from the water through our campsite only yards from us. Bears might have been less frightening. They were a cow and her adolescent bull calf. Not many creatures are more protective of their young. But before I could flinch they were gone.

That was enough for me, and I went to bed with a belly full of salmon and head spinning from Port. Close encounters of the "wild kind"; I didn't get scared until I stood and the Port hit me.

Jack shook me awake the next morning at 5 A.M., but I told him to bugger off and went back to sleep. My lids were still heavy from the Port. I woke again at 7 A.M. to the sound of rifle fire and remembered what Stan had said about opening day of Moose season. I gave no thought to the fact that we were in a state park where hunting is illegal. Roused by the gunfire, I slithered out of the cab-over bunk, made coffee, and dressed as quickly as my Port-over would allow. While I readied, Earwig lay deep in the throes of somnambulated flatulence. The RV stank. I got out quick before the vapors augmented the size of my Port head.

Jack was easy to find. It just took me awhile to walk upriver to him. He was standing in the river above the Picnic Hole in front of Stan's shop where the county road bridge spans the river. I sauntered up slowly to be sure I didn't spook any fish. Jack doesn't like it when his fish are spooked. He was inches upstream of the bridge.

"Doing any good?" I whispered from the water's edge behind him. He reeled in and stepped back to join me

"Cahill, you're never gonna' believe this."

"What?"

"About 7 o'clock I was working the water below the bridge and I made 2 casts when the same two Moose from last night crossed right below me."

He pointed to a spot downstream of the bridge and across the river, choked with alder.

"They worked their way over to this side, eating as they came. I figured I'd better move upstream and give them some room. They're kind of dangerous, especially a cow with a calf. So I moved upriver next to the bridge in case she charged and I had to run. I stood there watching them."

He pointed again.

"I really didn't want to turn my back on them and fish. As I'm watching, I heard a loud crack and the cow dropped in the river. Just fifty feet downstream of me! The bull calf went nuts running around its dead mother. Then, I saw a guy, with his rifle opposite me on the bridge, stand up and start to cross."

He pointed again.

"I kept still for a bit because the bull calf was seriously irritated, and somebody just dropped a moose next to me. I was a little freaked until the bull ran off. Just as I gathered my wits, this guy stepped into the river above the bridge and scared the hell out of me. He said he didn't see me and apologized if he wrecked the fishing. Then he started gutting it, right there."

Again he pointed to the ankle-deep slack water below the bridge.

"That's the end of fishing for today," I carped, referring to the blood's effect on the sensitive Salmon olfactory. They would hold until all trace of that was gone. I stared at the mound of guts in the shallow water.

"I wondered what that was when I walked up. So what happened?"

"I snuck around this side of the bridge and went into Stan's and asked him if he saw it. He didn't know what I was talking about. When I told him, he jumped up, ran to the window with his binoculars mumbling that he hadn't heard a shot. Then he got excited and called the Fish & Game. I guess the guy is a notorious poacher. Stan said they've been trying to bust him for twenty years. Then we waited for a good bit while the guy continued skinning. Stan was getting antsy. The ranger hadn't shown up yet and the hide was nearly off."

Jack took a deep breath and continued.

"Stan asked if he told the ranger a moose was shot in the river. And I said, 'No, you just said a moose was down in the river.' So he called the ranger back and said the magic word, 'shot'. The ranger was there in about two shakes. He cuffed the guy in his truck and came over to get our help loading the carcass and hide. I told him I saw the whole thing. He asked me to meet him for an interview at Stan's after lunch. He said the guy was so drunk he shouldn't be fishing let alone driving or shooting, and didn't even know where he was. The ranger wrote him up for DUI, illegal discharge of a firearm, reckless endangerment 'cause I was so close, shooting from the road and poaching in the park. The guy is screwed, and the ranger towed his pickup. He's screwed-big time. You shoulda' got up, Cahill. You missed out—totally. They're gonna' fly me back up here to testify."

"Crap!" It was all I could think to say.

We walked back to the RV to fix some breakfast. Earwig was just waking. The confined space smelled of man exhaust. Jack told the story all over again while opening the windows and roof vents.

"Why didn't you wake me?" Earwig complained. "I didn't hear any shot."

"Precisely!" Jack agreed.

"Crap!" Earwig protested.

We fussed around for the remainder of the morning, and about noon walked upriver to Stan's for Jack's meeting. The ranger said he already had a subpoena in the works. Arraignment, plea and trial date would trigger the subpoena process. He said he hoped it would be sometime in September. Jack looked at me. I could read his mind from the twinkle in the eye of a dead pan face.

"Steelhead fishing is pretty good about then," the ranger winked. With the interview over, Earwig sidled up to him.

"Officer can I ask one question?" he said.

"Go ahead," the cop replied.

In a dead-on Boris Badinoff impersonation, he spit out the question.

"Vhat squirrel do, now moose dead?"

The ranger did not find it amusing, but we busted a gut. The State of Alaska flew Jack to Anchorage on a round trip ticket, which he promptly changed the return for a later date. After he testified at the poacher's trial, which amounted to about ten minutes in the courtroom, he rented a car and drove down to meet Stan on the Anchor for a few days of steelhead fishing.

He called on his cell from there to gloat.

"You shoulda' got up, Cahill."

"Crap!" I told him.

# Drift 9

# Wha'd he take?

It seems as I get older, selecting a fly is less important than remembering to bring any. But there was a time when having the correct flies in my vest was probably more important than going fishing. I suffered from the intemperance of youth then. So my vest was always full of whatever I had so feverishly tied the night or week before. I really hate tying flies the night before. It seems adverse to the whole reason for fly fishing. It's not one of those rush-around sports. So spending the night before in frenetic hook-wrapping has a detracting effect on the actual fishing. Still, whether one ties or buys, the question always exists—what fly?

I'm serious when I say that looking in the bins of any fly shop makes my head spin. The rows upon rows of imposters, tied so perfectly, cry out, "Buy me! I'm the one." I'll stand there for what seems an eternity, cloaked in the shame of indecision. A clerk or guide asks if he can help. "With what?" is always my first thought. "Can you refocus my eyes?" Even if I take the advice of the shop staff it is no guarantee for success. They're in business to sell flies. I'm not inferring that fly shop guys will say anything to make a sale, but those flies have a pretty good profit margin. That's why they call it a fly shop. I haven't seen one yet whose sign proclaims, "Advice Shop or Wading Shop". A guy can drop a pocketful of cash in a real hurry, especially if advice is offered and taken during the perusal. No, I'm afraid it's all about the flies, which is only right. You can't fly fish without flies.

I have learned the importance of having a plan when entering a fly shop. I do not seek advice on fly selection. Frankly, I regret every piece of advice I have ever taken. Oh, you can ask polite directions, river flows and access points, where to eat and such, but do not ask about flies. It will only confuse the issue. Because if they don't have the #14 White Wulff you want, they will probably try to sell you a #14 Sparkle White Wulff or a Parachute Wulff. Those are just as good. Aren't they? As Zorro's father advised him, "Get in, make your 'Z' and get out". It's how I buy all my dry flies. They're too hard to tie. I tie nymphs and wet flies because they're what I mostly use.

When Jack and I approached the door of the Fox Creek Fly Shop on southern Colorado's Conejos River one brilliant September morning, he stepped in front of me, put his hand on the knob and blocked my entry.

"Look, Cahill, let's just buy what we need and get on the river. I don't want you making any new friends in here," he said referring to my proclivity towards the verbose.

I agreed and went right to work gathering my necessaries: a few dry flies that I didn't need but felt compelled to possess. He struck up a conversation with the shop staff the instant his foot hit the carpet.

Forty-five minutes later I dragged him to the front door, with the staff ebullient over his presence and despondent about his departure.

"Great to meet you, Jack-come on back for a beer when you guys are done."

So much for getting in and out or making any Z's, but while he distracted them with witty conversation, I made my selections without advice or interference.

The thing about flies is that they are a mystery. The patterns that one thinks look so good and buggy are not necessarily right for any given day. The patterns that seem overly simple are often a better choice. Even a piece of fuzz wrapped on a hook can out-entice the fanciest looking store bought pattern. I call that particular pattern an APM, (All Purpose Midge). It is any color dubbing material twisted around a #18 or #20 hook, ribbed with gold or silver wire. It's that simple and that effective. The APM has saved many a day on many a river. Yet when asked by the observing angler, even my careful explanation is often met with disbelief. APM's cannot be purchased in a fly shop. As far as I know, I am the only tier of that pattern. It's no wonder other anglers think I'm flip. I get the same response of disbelief when using a Grand Dad. Just telling the name to another angler results in that look-the, "I think you're a smart ass" look. It's a fly I discovered in the tackle of an English friend who came to Colorado with his Grand Dad's fly kit. I didn't invent it; I just tried it. Now I use them all the time. I guess the mystery is that they can't be found in fly shops. They are an old English Sedge pattern, meant to be fished wet. Sedge is what the English call caddis. The Grand Dad is quite simple and devastatingly effective. It is comprised of a flat gold tinsel body, a brown hen neck, soft hackle, and turkey feather bits for wings. I can crank them out by the hundreds because they take so little time to tie. But even simpler patterns are available for the angler who takes the time to look.

Once, Jack and I spent a day frothing the waters of the upper Frying Pan above Ruedi Reservoir, on that river's South Fork. Moments before dusk, we were tired and frustrated but decided to try a section just above the confluence of the North and South Forks before giving up for the day. Reaching the water I snapped off the fly I had been using for the last several hours-my last fly. I asked Jack for one but he was out. We didn't have a lot of money in those days, and neither of us tied back then, so we were lucky to have five or six flies each when starting out on any given day. We had lost them all that day, but Jack had some gold bait hooks in his vest and we each tied one on. I threaded a cigarette butt on mine and pulled a little of the filter material out to trail like a shuck pattern. He stuck a dandelion bud on his. It seemed stupid, but fish were rising and we weren't ready to quit. We had to catch at least one fish. As I said, we were younger then.

On the first drift I hooked up to a nice trout, and continued to do so until I could find no more butts in my vest and it was too dark for Jack see a dandelion bud. The day ended with the profit of knowing that we didn't need anything other than our wits to catch fish. The fish were rising and splashing as we walked to the truck. It was a good day. I haven't fished with a cigarette butt or a dandelion bud since, even with the knowledge that I could. It now seems demeaning to the fish, not to mention any other anglers within sight who might ask that age-old question, "What did he take?" How can I say it was a Camel Light butt? Such a response might start a fight. Fisticuffs have resulted for far lesser reasons; so much for the gentility of the sport.

The fact is, over the years I have learned to keep my response to their inquiries less than truthful. It saves time and feelings. I say only that it's a wet fly—caddis, mayfly, midge or nymph. When they ask to see it—I show them. They can search the fly shops forever and not find it. It keeps them off the river for awhile anyway.

I must confess to the intentional misuse of flies. I like to fish dry flies under the surface. I know it sounds counterproductive, but it works. I discovered this quite by accident one day while fishing the Lake Fork of the Gunnison. While on a camping trip to the upper Rio Grande with my wife and t(w)eenage daughter, I stopped at one of the many public access points along its course on the road to Lake City. They needed a break and while they stretched I took the opportunity to flick a fly. My rod was rigged with a #14 Light Cahill dry fly so I grabbed it, leaving my vest and waders in the truck. I had time for only a dozen casts before they were ready to resume the ride over Slumgullion Pass and down the other side into the Rio Grande valley above Creede. The water next to the highway pull off was a classic break-and-riffle configuration with an inviting pool between the two. I cast the Light Cahill into the water above the drop and let it drift over the surface of the pool and down through the riffle, as a natural bug would. The fly was buoyant, staying on the surface quite well. I could see fish holding in the depths of the little pool, but they had no interest in the floating delicacy above them. By the fifth or sixth cast the fly was waterlogged and sank without hesitation. That's when the big rainbow hit. I saw it clearly. It chased the fly downstream through the little pool and caught it at the tail with a voracious chomp. From that moment on, I was hooked. Now, even in the height of dry fly season, I will fish them wet, unless I actually see surface action. And more often than not I fish them wet, regardless. This practice has caused some disdain among my fishing companions, especially if I am out-catching them. And one day on northern Idaho's Wood River my admission to it was the source for a good laugh.

Jack and I had driven from the McCloud River in northern California to Ketchum, Idaho to attend an old friend's wedding. I was to meet my wife, who drove from Colorado for the event. We arrived a day early to take advantage of the Wood before the festivities. The Wood is a marvelous river with numerous access points along its course south of Ketchum. As always, I started to fish with a wet fly rig and a nymph dropper. We plied the water in our standard hopscotch technique by skipping over each other from hole or run to hole or run, occasionally leaving several between us. In some instances we had to bump up above other anglers already on the river. There were quite a few others that day and eventually Jack and I became separated by some distance, with anglers between us. I had caught several nice fish on the wet fly and nymph rig I was running, but the day became progressively slower. Finally the action stopped altogether. Even the other anglers weren't catching anything.

I approached a large run well above Jack's position with two guys fishing it, fully intent on moving upstream beyond them. As I approached the usual greetings and inquiries ensued and they offered the hole to me.

"We've got to go," they invited. "Not that you'll do any good; we haven't caught a thing."

I thanked them and let the spot settle down a bit by changing my rig to a single dry fly with a small split shot above. While I waited, other anglers I had passed moved upstream to occupy the run directly below me. Satisfied that I had let the pool settle enough to fish, I stood and began dead drifting the fly from the run's head to the tail below. Low bushes and limbs overhung the opposite side, and I knew if I could get the fly to drift under that cover, I would probably hook up. The cast was a difficult one, and required hitting the water above the pool close to the bank with a well-timed upstream mend to prevent the fast water between myself and the opposite bank from ripping the fly. It took me a number of tries to get it placed right, and then a subsequent number of practice mends, but I finally got the drift.

Like magic, when the mended cast brought the fly under the limbs it was hammered by a well-endowed fish. I could tell it was a big fish by the way it manhandled me, even before it broke water. I had to act quick, getting it on the reel before it dragged my line into the limbs or, worse yet, went airborne under them. Somehow I managed to persuade the big fish from under the overhanging limbs and into the open, but faster, water of the run. That's when it broke the surface with a dazzling aerial and revealed itself as a 20 inch rainbow. A fight ensued for some minutes before I was able to wear it down enough to land and release it.

I noticed from the corner of my eye that the anglers below had stopped to watch.

I wanted Jack to know what had transpired and how well I had done with the drowned dry fly, that he might benefit from such knowledge. It's a thing fishing buddies do for each other. I wanted to brag a little as well, so I headed downstream to where he fished below the w'anglers. That's what I call anglers who watch you catch a fish: watching anglers—w'anglers. He happened to see me coming and started walking upstream. We met where the w'anglers were still unproductively working their run.

"Hey, that looked like a pretty big fish you had up there." one of the two said to me.

"Yeah, that was a good rainbow. I think close to 20 inches," I replied.

"What did he take?" the other angler asked.

I knew they hadn't caught anything and were hoping for some advice that might improve their luck.

"That was on a #18 BWO-Wulff," I offered.

"A dry fly?" the same guy queried. "We've been fishing dry flies and I haven't seen anything rise all day," he added.

"Well, it wasn't exactly dry. I sunk it," I admitted.

"Are you kidding?"

"No," I said, showing him the fly with split shot above, while Jack stood to the side listening in.

"I'll be damned," the guy said.

His buddy also stood by listening to our exchange, while I explained that I fished it like a nymph.

"I have to try that, but I have just one question."

"What's that?" I said.

"How will I know when I catch one?"

Jack laughed out loud and said, "You'll know, pal."

We chuckled about that the rest of the day. Jack says it every time we start fishing.

"How will I know again?"

But the best inquiry I have yet to hear was on a stretch of the Roaring Fork at a place called Hook's Bridge. There, above the bridge, is a large pool fed by a deep channel adjacent to the road. It's in the lower part of the valley below the confluence with the Frying Pan River, so the water is a little warmer in the winter and allows for a place to start fishing as early as February. In fact, it is one of the spots we usually fish during that time of the year. The days are short then, and provide only a small window of time where both the angler and the fish are comfortable.

Jack and I met up there one February day to get a jump on the Spring fishing season. It's easy access, and no trudge along a snow-covered trail is required because of its proximity to the road. Cabin fever had a terrible grip on me. Jack started calling to complain about his case in January. The fishing license I had purchased right after the New Year was burning a hole in my vest. We agreed that since the ice was off the river, there really was no reason to stay home and watch TV when we could fish Hook's Bridge.

As usual, I took one side of the deep feeder channel and he the other. We worked it thoroughly for quite a while, but failed to produce even a single strike. The sun was getting low and the temperature becoming a bit chill, bordering on uncomfortable. Just as I was about to say "Uncle" and tell Jack I'd had enough, I noticed my fly line had stopped moving along with the current. It's a sure sign either that something has taken the fly or that it's snagged on the bottom. I set the hook by raising the rod. Whatever had my fly moved downstream, taking line from my reel. This can be the sign of a big fish that is hooked but doesn't know it yet. I set the hook again to make sure. Again it moved a few feet downstream.

"OK, a big whitefish," I thought.

Whitefish often don't break water and can be powerful adversaries in such fast current. I began to draw in the line by raising my rod and reeling as I reset it. The fish was coming along with it—another sign of a big whitefish. Soon I had the thing close enough to see a large silver gray presence in the water 15 or 20 feet downstream of my position.

Now I was sure it was a big Whitefish. We were fishing a mile a so upstream of where the state record for Whiteys, a five or six pounder, was taken only a few years before. I was elated. I knew I had something big on and as it had yet to break water, I was convinced I had the new state record.

With my arm seizing from rod pumping and reeling, I finally got the thing to my feet. I was aghast at the sight on the end of my line.

"What the hell is it?" Jack yelled from across the channel.

I really couldn't believe my eyes. It wasn't a state record. In fact it wasn't a whitefish at all.

"It's a dead lamb," I yelled back

"What did he take?" Jack asked.

# Drift 10

# Her Stinky Beaver

There is a river on an uninhabited island in southeast Alaska. The Nellie Martin empties into Patton Bay on its southwest coast. It is at the very top of the Japan current. At least one of everything crossing the Pacific Ocean ends up on the South coast of it, including the vessels. The shipwrecks are interesting. But the diversity and plethora of ordinary things is fascinating. I cannot imagine how some of it gets there. Things like an automatic coffee maker, a new trash can with the lid and label still on it, twenty-foot 2 x 4's, were everywhere on the beach, well mixed among a continuous jumble of logs and tree trunks on the shore of Patton Bay. I found a four-foot fluorescent tube stuck by its prongs in a log, unbroken. On the river is a Forest Service cabin large enough to cozily house four guests. The Forest Service calls them guests.

Jack and I were to meet Mudge and his college friend Barstool in Anchorage to catch the early morning flight for Cordova. Mudge was delayed getting out of Colorado, and we met Barstool without him.

After some quick introductions, Jack and I boarded the flight with our brand new buddy Barstool. We had never seen him before, but we couldn't just leave him. He was supposed to go with us anyway, so we had to make him a buddy. It was the only way around the awkward situation. We had a whole day and a half in Cordova before our flight to the island. Our billet for two nights was an old cannery complex. The place is wonderful. We stayed in a turn of the century house. The employee barracks are on the second floor of the administration building and in a state of complete preservation. Even the kitchen table was set with the wares of those times. An immense warehouse loomed over the little cove, and inside a boat the size of a small house lay heeled over. It consumed only a small portion of the floor area of that gigantic building. And of course there was the old cannery itself, docks and the like. It is a very nostalgic place and reeks of an earlier time when such places fed the working classes of America.

We checked in, stashed our goods, donned our waders and drove the rental car out to the first fishing shop we saw. We asked where to fish, not about flies.

"You passed it on the way in from the airport."

As I remember, the river had not seen a salmon run for some years. So this run was unexpected and prolific. We parked with the dozens of other cars in the ditches on either side of the bridge spanning the river. All the fishermen were downstream of it. We thought the upstream side more inviting, and began the rigging ritual after perusing the scene. Jack finished first and started for the river. I was a blink from a clean getaway, when Barstool cried out. He stood holding out his hand with a #2 Alaska Maryanne sticking in his thumb, very deep past the barb. It was a bad one and close to the joint.

"Oh! Man, are you kidding?" I complained aloud.

"Can you get it out?" he pleaded.

"Maybe, but it's gonna' hurt, 'cause while I'm doing this, he's catching his limit," I said pointing to Jack. "And then he'll start working on ours."

So there I stood next to a river in Alaska that was having its best salmon run in years, Jack was already fishing, and I'm taking a hook out of a guy I just met a few hours earlier.

I looked his thumb over carefully. Then grabbing the big #2 with my hemostats, I shoved it through his thumb has hard as I could. With the tip through and exposed, I flattened the barb, but made sure to tweak it a little. He winced, twitched involuntarily and cursed allowed

"Jesus!" he protested.

"Hold still. This is the one that will hurt." I assured him.

My intent was to extol some payment for the delay of his carelessness

Tweaking the hook one last time I jerked it out with my hemostats. Dropping the fly, I walked as fast as I could to the river. Jack had three on the bank by the time I had wet the fly. But I had a good afternoon. Barstool got skunked.

That night we discussed our day and plans for picking up Mudge, how we could fish the bridge spot before his flight arrived, and gather our provisions before the afternoon flight to Montague Island. We dined at the Reluctant Fisherman right on the harbor. I can recall only a few better nights in a restaurant.

The morning found us much refreshed and ready for a quick fish before Mudge's flight arrived. After breakfast at the Reluctant again, we headed the rental car back to the highway bridge. During the rig and dress ritual, I discovered my reel missing. Jack and Barstool walked to the river. I jumped in the rental car and drove to the old cannery. My mind's eye could see it on the dresser in my room. By the time I returned to the river, Jack and Barstool had their limits on the bank and it was time to pick up Mudge and take a bush flight to the Nellie Martin. I got skunked without even fishing.

Our pilot was a middle-aged lady. Because Barstool was the new guy, on his first Alaska trip, he was offered the right seat next to her. It's the best view from a De Haviland Beaver. We sat cramped in the rear seat with our gear and supplies against the back of our heads. Flying in a Beaver is tantamount to sitting in an empty dumpster while it is beaten. You can't hear a thing except the big rotary engine.

But the cockpit and cabin are tight and you can smell a lot. At first, I thought the aroma was part of the aircraft's patina. As we flew in the deafening tin can, the smell became stronger. Somebody had a potent and unfortunate gas attack. I knew I couldn't talk to Jack or Mudge, so I elbowed Jack hard in the ribs to get his attention. He gave me a shot back. I looked him in the eye with my thumb and index finger pinching my nose, and then gave him the cut it sign, thumb slashing my throat. He shook his head in abject denial and pointed to Mudge on his left. Jack's elbow got his attention and we both repeated the accusation in sign language—abject and indignant denial this time. Mudge pointed to the front seat. I leaned forward a bit placing my head next to the back of Barstool's head rest. Whew-wee it stunk up there! I jerked myself back in the seat as far as I could. My head slammed against the stowed gear. I looked at Jack and Mudge while straightening my hat. They had their t-shirt collars pulled up over their noses. The fabric vibrated in and out with each breath, like the diaphragm on a speaker. I pulled mine up as well, preferring the smell of my own halitosis. We rode most of the eighty-five-minute trip like that, signing back and forth our disgust for Barstool's thoughtless relief of himself.

Finally and gratefully, we landed on a stretch of beach just adjacent to an old gravel landing strip. Why the pilot didn't use the strip, I don't know. If she had it would have saved us a good mile of hauling gear to the cabin. By then we were too nauseous to ask. We barreled out of that Beaver like it was on fire. I swear the faintest wisp of vapor wafted from the open aircraft doors. We stood there dumbfounded and lightheaded, waiting for the air to clear before we dared unload.

A Beaver can hold a lot. By the time we had it all out, there was an imposing pile on the beach. The pilot fired up the aircraft and swung it around for takeoff, only to get stuck in the soft sand. She signaled us for a push and we obliged. The big round beach tires were buried to the hubs, and it took some effort on our part and considerable throttle on hers, and the thing climbed out of the holes the tires were in and up on to the hard-packed area of the beach. She throttled back the engine to idle and waved us over to the cockpit through the open window.

"The cabin is about a mile and half west on the trail off the end of the old runway. Sorry I can't get you any closer. I'll be back on Tuesday about 2 P.M, weather permitting. If it's a bad weather day don't haul your gear back down here. Stay in the cabin. I'll come when the weather clears. Hope you guys brought enough food. Oh yeah, just in case no one mentioned it, this is the place where Fish & Game puts the problem bears. So you might see a few. If you have an emergency—there's a logging camp about six miles west on the road. Just follow the river trail up to the confluence—you'll see the bridge," she said.

With that, she closed the cockpit window and gunned the engine. The Beaver lurched under the thunderous application of throttle. She rolled down the beach a short way and was airborne. Those Beavers hop right into the air.

We stood looking at the pile of gear and coolers, and then back at each other, then at the Beaver, now just a dot above the horizon, its engine barely audible. The silence reminded me of where I was. Nothing is more lonesome than standing on some wilderness spot next to a big pile of gear, listening to the sound of your ride fading in the distance, especially if your ride just advised you to "watch out that you don't get killed". We had to carry it all a mile and a half.

We began to sort the gear, don packs and sling dry bags. I found an 8-foot length of 2x4 on the beach to use as a Mombosa Stick for carrying the coolers porter style to the cabin. As I threaded the lumber through the handles, Barstool assisted. I could not restrain myself from broaching the subject of his putrefying flatulence in the confined space of that aircraft.

"That wasn't me," he denied emphatically.

"Bullshit. It wasn't me!" we three chimed in unison.

"I didn't say it was," Barstool retorted-feeling, I am sure, like the new guy finding himself in the position of defending his veracity.

"It was our pilot."

"Bullshit!" We chimed together.

"No really—it was her breath—I know—I'm a dentist," he said with authority

We rode him about that for the next 5 days, trying to blame that sweet middle aged lady. We were brutal and relentless.

On Tuesday when she touched down, I opened the cockpit door to greet her and was stung by the aroma. We played paper, rock and scissors to see who got the front seat and the full brunt of it. I lost. As she gunned the aircraft engine and careened over the sand for takeoff, I turned my head to look back at my 3 companions. Each had his nose covered with his t-shirt collar—see no evil—speak no evil—and smell no evil. They gave me the thumbs up.

When we got back to Cordova we had to buy Barstool's dinner at the Reluctant for doubting him and busting his chops for 5 days.

Man, that old gal had a stinky Beaver.

# Drift 11
# The Gau Lieter of Nellie Martin

When the lady bush pilot departed, our day's work had just begun. We loaded ourselves with packs, and dry bags plus a cooler on the Mombosa Stick. It was a slow mile and half walk, with frequent stops. About a mile from the beach, we encountered a man in hip waders standing some fifteen feet below the trail, on the river's edge. He waved a fly rod back and forth in a false casting motion. Unintelligible speech came from his lips.

"Vee aire Chermun und vee aire fleigen," He yelled barely audible over the tumult of the river.

We waved and kept walking. A few yards up the trail from the rod waver was a break in the alder thicket that skirted the old air strip. Through the break we could see a tent camp with five men standing around a fire, a lot of smoke and no flame. They waved and repeated the rod waver's greeting, through the smoke curtain. We waved and kept slogging. We made three trips apiece that day, amounting to nine miles each. It was a brutal day, and late in the evening before we had the cabin set up for housekeeping. All we could do was eat and go to bed.

At 6 A.M., next, we woke to the sound of large-caliber pistol reports and the shrill chirp of referee whistles. We bolted from our wooden bunks and ran for the cabin's entry deck. Jack grabbed the 12-gauge on the way out. We stood there in long handles and bare feet while the reports and whistles grew steadily closer. It came from upstream, on the river trail that passed through the cabin clearing right in front of our porch. About 25 yards past the cabin it dove into the dark and dank Alaskan woods. We stepped off the porch and looked up the trail. All we could see was the privy door swinging in the morning breeze. The shots and whistle chirps continued; growing closer with each passing second. We moved to the yard, looking intently.

Eventually, a man emerged from the dark tunnel at the forest's edge. He was running full tilt with two Silver Salmon in his arms, clutching a fly rod in one hand. The whistle clenched in his teeth chirped in rhythm with his heavy breathing. The salmon seemed to bobble in sync with his gait. Behind him five more men in the same comic quick step followed, all carrying salmon in their arms and chirping a cacophony. The last man was firing what looked like a .45 caliber revolver over his shoulder as he ran. He was followed by a large brown bear. The bear was close, but only trotting to keep up. At the sight of the bear we stepped back on the porch to make way. All except for Jack, who stood his ground barefoot and long john clad. He chambered a round into the breach of the pump 12-gauge and yelled to the chirping men.

"Throw it a fish!"

They did not seem to understand, and kept running and chirping their way through the clearing and on past the cabin. The second man in line bobbled a fish from his tentative grip. It hit the ground about 40 feet in front of us. The bear nearly overtook the shooter, but it saw or smelled the fish and stopped to retrieve it. That was all it really wanted, and with a fish securely in the grip of that powerful maw, it turned and slowly ambled back into the forest. The men continued on through the clearing back to their camp. We could hear the whistles chirping until they were out of sight. I was thankful the last guy in line had stopped shooting.

With the men out of sight, we stood looking up the trail where the bear had gone and down the trail where the men had run. I don't think any of us wanted to go up that trail to fish. Breakfast and rigging were conducted in the exaggerated pace of retirees. We couldn't move slowly enough. We weren't in any hurry to go out there. None cared to admit such to the others. I had never taken an entire morning to rig, but I did that day. Regardless, I was the first one ready.

"We're right behind you," Jack said.

"No way am I going up there alone, without the 12-gauge and you guys. I at least, need somebody to outrun," I quipped.

"Did you see those morons? Who carries fish in their arms like that—and what about the whistles? And what the hell did that guy think he was gonna' hit, firing like that?" I pondered aloud while hooking a small canister of bear mace to my wader belt.

"That was bizarre, alright." Jack said. "One of those problem bears, I guess."

Before we finished our prep the tent campers came sheepishly along the trail and emerged into the clearing. They stood in pseudo formation in front of the cabin porch were we sat. They were stiff. It seemed that introductions would ensue. None did. Only a proclamation in halting English was offered. The stiffest guy I'd ever seen said, "Dat Bear iz baad."

"Ja!" The others concurred in unison. With that they broke ranks and headed up the trail to the confluence.

"OK, that was strange," I said. "I think those guys are German."

"Ja," Jack agreed. "Let's go up there and see "vas ist los."

We gathered our accoutrements du jour and strolled up the menacing forest trail. Jack took the point with the twelve-gauge and I the drag, my trusty can of pepper spray on my belt and a big horse pistol tucked deep in the bib of my waders. It was a treacherous walk. The trail was wet, slippery and well shaded. Roots and deadfall made the walk slow going. After about a mile of torment and angst, we came upon the confluence of the river and a smaller stream. The Germans were well positioned in the available water the confluence offered. It formed a big holding pool; fifty yards above it were the logging road and the bridge spanning the Nellie Martin. Five of the Germans stood downstream of the big pool, and one was above in the flat water. We stood for a time watching them fish, discussing the water. They had the river fairly blocked and there was no room for us to fish. Ten anglers around that pool would not work.

The river below the pool was not crossable or fishable, and the only way to get above the tent men was to cross the small stream above its juncture with the main river. The turbid little stream was the Patton

River. It ran for the confluence pool in a fright, a big flume of knee-deep water racing for the sea. The Germans had strung a stout rope to trees on either side of its banks. Jack made the attempt first. It proved doable and we followed. It was a bold wade despite my death grip on the swaying rope. The moment we made the opposite bank and were in good position to get upstream of the Germans, the bear appeared on the opposite bank of the river. The Germans below the confluence bolted and ran for their camp, leaving their lone companion upstream and in the middle of the river. The large bear was too close for him to continue fishing. Sincere discomfort twisted his face. We urged him to come onto the little spit that jutted into the confluence on which we stood. He waddled tentatively towards us, looking over his shoulder at the bear with every step.

As the bear stepped into the water so did Jack, to assist the rattled angler. The bear stayed put while we took the man across the little stream. It was the second time I had to cross the damn thing in the passing of only minutes, and we had yet to fish. We surmised the guy was a little upset on the walk to the cabin, chiefly by his utterances. He said little that made sense while walking back, except "Danke" when he left us. Miraculously, the bear didn't follow. They were definitely German. I felt sorry for the guy because his buddies had bailed on him.

Later that afternoon we returned to the confluence hole to enjoy our first attempt at fishing. We stationed ourselves as pairs, above and below the sweet spot. The fishing was slow and only a few errant Pink Salmon were caught and released. Although fun to catch, they were not the prey we sought. The next day we tried the big hole in front of the cabin and the confluence hole again with the same result. It seemed the Silvers had yet to arrive—the chance that comes with the price of admission.

On the third day I slept late and woke to find the cabin empty. After a quick cup of bad coffee, I dressed and rigged. The cabin hole was unoccupied. I made the spooky walk up the forest trail, to find my three companions stationed as before at the confluence pool. There was no sign of the Germans. I stepped into the water below the big pool next to Mudge. Jack and Barstool were on the topside of the hole. Just as I began to pay line out into the current for a cast, I heard noise from the bank behind me, and turned in the direction of the source. I knew before looking. Our bear sauntered out from the dank forest onto the gravel bar along the river's edge. The damn thing was only 20 yards from us. Mudge and I had nowhere to go but the main current. We were trapped. He began throwing his hands in the air to make himself larger while yelling at the bear.

"HO! BEAR!"

It took another few steps in our direction. I joined in and threw a few baseball size rocks, to punctuate my "Ho Bears". I dropped my rod, drew my pistol and pepper spray. I didn't want to spray or shoot it. First, a pistol round would have to be very well placed to kill, and second, I didn't think I could place one that well. I had heard the stories about Alaskan bears shaking off a pistol shot, or the shots bouncing off their skull. And I sure didn't want it close enough to spray. Most of all I did not care to have a pissed-off bear on my hands.

I turned to Mudge for advice. He stood holding a police rated crowd fogger. It was a three-pound fire extinguisher of pepper spray. Really, it said "Crowd" on the label. It fired 35 feet. It was wind and rain rated. It was a big nasty can of bear mace and he was dying to use it. Just so long as I didn't die for him to use it. The bear took a few more steps in our direction.

"Supposed to be good for 100 people", he said.

From behind us, across the big pool, I heard the metallic click of a shotgun shell being chambered. Bingo! That did the trick. The bear high tailed back into the woods. Mudge stood poised, fogger at the ready. We nervously returned to fishing. But our efforts were halfhearted and we quit after an hour. Giving the bear some time to amble away seemed prudent. While Mudge and I waited on the trail for the others to make the treacherous wade across the Patton River, we heard the faint sound of pistol reports coming from the direction of the cabin and the Germans' camp. Mudge stood, clutching the noxious canister. I cautiously took the point along the dark trail to the cabin. Upon entering the clearing, I noticed the privy was on its side. Rattled by the sight, I called for Jack to come up with the shotgun. We crept with short little steps to the front of the cabin, weapons drawn and cocked. Mudge cowered behind us, crowd fogger at the ready, no doubt aimed at my back. If the bear jumped out, I just knew he was going to hit me with a cloud of acrid gas. On the porch, our solar shower bag hung bitten and torn. Large, muddy paw prints covered the front window and door. Our gear, rod tubes and such were scattered across the little porch, and the fresh water collection barrel had been turned over. It was empty. At least the bear was gone. But it had wrecked the exterior of our camp.

It became clear what the gunshots were about when the German shooter stopped by to report that the bear had paid their camp a visit. He described pepper spraying it from just a few yards while it pillaged their camp.

"The thing just shook it off," he said in much better English.

He was visibly upset. At least we had a stout wooden structure in which to hide. They had only tents and their wits. The latter seemed somewhat lacking, considering the earlier exhibition of their bear craft. I think they drew lots, sending him as an emissary to feel out our position on them moving in. Jack said no.

"Not till at least two of them get eaten."

The loss of fresh drinking water was a problem. Rain water collected from the roof was funneled by a gutter into a large plastic trash barrel; now overturned. But the sky was clear. We needed water now and couldn't wait for the next rain. Granted it rains frequently in southeast Alaska, but it wasn't going to rain right then. Jack and I took the ceramic water filter and collapsible water jug to the river. There we began the tedious task of filtering enough water to get us by until it rained. It takes some time to filter three to five gallons through one of those things. We took turns pumping, cleaning the filter, and holding the water can. Mudge and Barstool stayed behind to straighten the camp.

Back at the cabin we found the place well organized with our rod tubes and other gear resting neatly on the deck against the cabin wall. I carried the water into the cabin. When I touched the door handle, I knew something was amiss. My palm began to burn and itch. Outside, Jack was rummaging through his rod tubes to make sure no rod tips were broken by the bear's mauling. He spewed a stream of curses. I stepped out to see what had prompted his tirade.

"My eyes and ears are burning like hell," he complained.

"My hand, too." I said.

"Oh! Sorry, you guys. I sprayed all that down to keep the bear off the porch," Mudge said lifting his crowd fogger from the ground next to the fire, where he sat on a log biscuit.

"You moron!" I castigated him. "I'm glad I didn't have to pee."

It took several more trips to the river to wash the gear and carry buckets of water back to wash the deck and door. We never did get the stuff off the door.

The next day we encountered seals in the cabin hole during the incoming morning tide. Because the tide had filled the river channel with so much sea water, it was difficult to fish. We decided to try the confluence hole after lunch, and stationed ourselves as before, two men up and two down. I stood knee-deep in the water and worked the big pool with an Egg Sucking Leach. It was difficult to get a drift, and ripping the fly was the only option. After five or six casts, a seal rose just yards from me and barked. Moments later I hooked into a big male Silver. The fish ripped me good. After a bit, it tired and I gained enough control to land it. To my surprise the sea-bright beauty had a large bite out of its sterling flank—the seal. I released the fish. It had been through enough. Things began to take shape in my mind. I called to Jack on the upstream side of the big pool.

"That big male had a huge bite out of its side. I think the seals are driving them upstream"

The seals couldn't pass the big pool because of the sharp break that dumped into it, and because the tidal influence ended there.

Jack waded back to the bank and walked upstream to the logging road bridge. He climbed the steep bank adjacent to the abutments of railroad tie cribbing, and walked out to the center of the span. He lowered his cap brim to his eyebrows and cupped his hands around his eyes. Intently, he scanned the flat water on either side of the bridge.

"They're rocketing through here like deranged torpedoes," he called out.

Now things began to make sense. These salmon had seals hunting them all the way to the confluence pool. It was as far as the seals could go. But the fish continued hell-bent to spawn. They were moving upstream faster than any I had ever seen.

We returned to the cabin. Over cocktails and dinner we discussed our options. Because the fish weren't holding in the river around the cabin, two choices were available to us. We could go upstream of the bridge to find them, or we could try to fish them in the bay at the mouth of the river. Both had their drawbacks. Hell, they weren't running back to the ocean. But upstream meant dealing with the bear(s). We decided upstream was our best chance to find the fish.

In the morning the Germans stopped on their way upstream. Evidently our assistance to their abandoned companion earned us some respect points, because they suddenly spoke pretty good English. The shooter did the talking and was a little embarrassed for bolting at the sight of the bear. I didn't think him the worse for it. At least we could have a fishing conversation. His companions took formation as previously exhibited. He said they planned to day hike upstream of the bridge. Jack encouraged them to go and they did—in formation. Evidently the Germans had figured the river out as well.

"I thought we were going to fish that water today?" I scolded.

"We are," Jack said.

"Yeah, but now we have those guys up there with us," I stated.

"True, but how could we stop them? And if we wait for an hour or so they'll be a good mile or more above us and so will that horrible bear," Jack explained. "The way that thing is keyed in on fishermen it has to follow them, and we'll be shed of it all day. Fish or no, we won't have to contend with the son of a bitch today."

The plan seemed good and we took our time setting out. We packed lunches and tied a few flies, giving our competitors the time required to put on some distance. Knowing the bear was likely with our neighbors did nothing to ease my dread of walking the forest trail again-twice. I felt no shame in this, for fear is a healthy thing. The others felt the same, I am confident. Walk it we did.

Upstream of the bridge is a much different river. It is long and flat with ample cover, riffle and hole or pocket. But it is deep, and in fact crossings were the topic of debate-here or there, or why cross when there's nowhere to go? The banks were tree and alder lined. It was an adventure, as well as a serious hike in waders with packs, weapons, water and lunch. Mudge wasn't happy with the Crowd Fogger so he left it behind.

"The German said it was useless to spray it. It's been sprayed too many times." His inflection denoted some sympathy for the bear's plight. Besides he'd used most of it on the cabin.

"Does a hundred people, Cahill," kept going around my head like a line from a ditty. I could see him holding it up when he unpacked his gear. I can't believe they let you fly with things like that, back then. But they did.

I had no sympathy for the bear and carried the shotgun, willingly. It rained in curtains the whole long way. We never saw the bear, or the Germans. We saw all their tracks though. It was with them.

We were strategic angling geniuses. The calculated crossings, the scouting, even the lunch spot was selected so as best not to sully the water-all were expertly done. The sheer unmitigated brilliance of it all was intoxicating and we reveled in its light despite the sheets of driving rain. Our plan, so craftily conceived, took every tactic into account. All it lacked was fish. There were no fish! They had run upriver with the Germans—and the bear. The rain continued unabated the whole long way back.

At the cabin we hunkered down to get warm and dry from our day's march. With some hot coffee inside me, I made a trip to the cabin pool to put a marker stick at the water's edge. It was really raining. That close to the ocean the sheets and curtains of rain were more apparent and accentuated. It was exhilarating to be in. At least for a few minutes, knowing the cabin was only yards away, not miles. The Germans came back just at the gloaming. They were wet and hadn't found the fish until late in the day. That's when the bear had started to harass them, and they'd been force-marching back ever since. The bear stayed with the fish. But at least they'd found them.

We spent another day in the steady drizzle trying to gather enough firewood, like 2x4's and other dimensioned lumber, from the jetsam on the beach so we could keep the cabin warm and dry our gear. Regular logs on the beach are too wet and just don't burn. But the kiln dried stuff was a Godsend. Things don't dry so fast in Alaska and it was still raining in sheets.

The river rose four feet overnight. It was unapproachable, let alone fishable. Even the seals had retreated. We took turns walking the beach alone in search of 2 by's to keep the plant operating. That's when I found the 20 footer. Jack came back with a huge framing timber, very new, just off some ship. It hadn't even obtained a patina yet. We had to pass the Germans' camp each trip to the beach. They were gathered around a smoldering fire in the incessant rain. Like Harry Truman's jackass, all they could do was stand there and take it.

The day before pickup we leisurely fished the cabin hole. It rained so much the day and night before even it was hard to approach. The rain had stopped, but the sky was still thickly overcast. I wondered about the plane in weather like this. We satisfied ourselves with a day of catching and releasing pinks in the lower river at the cabin hole. The Germans joined us. The bear thankfully did not.

Pickup day dawned bright and clear and we were delighted to be leaving. The day required another nine mile per man effort with gear down to the beach. But the loads were lighter. The food was gone and the coolers held waders and boots now. We started right after breakfast and didn't finish until a half hour before pickup. The Germans were also breaking camp and piled their gear a few hundred yards further down the beach. They gave us deference because we had the longer hike. They were gentlemen.

As we waited for our ride we met between the two piles to say our goodbyes. The shooter complained that their pickup was two hours late, and how they had been left before. Their flight was out of Anchorage, some hundreds of miles further north than ours. We began to worry about ours.

"Two dayz dat son a bitch vouldn't comes," one of the others grumbled.

"If you guys get stuck, the cabin's empty and there's a full bottle of vodka on the shelf, and firewood," Jack offered."

After some minutes of polite chat, the faint but unmistakable drone of rescue broke the horizon. As it grew louder the Germans became ebullient and ran for their pile of gear. They stood waving, confident it was their ride. As the aircraft came closer they cheered. It landed on the beach and taxied up to our pile of gear. It was our lady bush pilot. Not the plane the Germans had expected. We had to push her out of the same holes in the sand before we loaded. The forlorn Germans stood by their pile of sodden gear as we raced along the beach. They didn't even wave.

From the banking Beaver, I saw the bear waddling down the beach towards them. The Germans grabbed what they could and ran for the cabin. I hope they found that bottle of Vodka.

The cabin on the Nelly Martin

# Drift 12

# The View From Abaft

Not too many years ago the popularity of McKenzie-style drift boats virtually clogged the Roaring Fork and Upper Colorado rivers. These boats were originally developed to run the famed and wild McKenzie River in Canada, which flows north from Lake Athabasca into the Beaufort Sea. They were the principal means of transportation available to prospectors seeking their fortunes in the gold fields of the Klondike. Since then, they have been modified to a smaller scale and adapted to running the less treacherous rivers of the west as a means of covering a great deal of water in a single day for the purpose of fishing—mostly fly fishing. On any given day in the summer, the rivers of the west are literally peppered with them and other craft.

By other craft, I mean just about anything that will float. I've seen people floating on inner tubes, air mattresses and homemade log rafts. I have floated the Gunnison and Rio Grande Rivers while sitting atop my belly boat, with the feet fins on my hands for oars and a fly rod tucked tightly between my knees. But the craft I saw while fishing the Middle Roaring Fork one day in midsummer gave me a good chuckle.

I looked up from the drift of my fly to see two younger fellows coming downstream in a kid pool. I'm not talking about one of those little inflatable kid pools, but rather on the hard extruded plastic kind—the big one, maybe eight feet in diameter. Each held a canoe paddle. If that wasn't comical enough, it got better when they tried to guide the craft. It really didn't matter what they did with the paddles because the pool had no keel or spline, nor did it have a bow or stern. Each time they dipped a paddle, the pool spun wildly like a top, first one direction then the other.

I could tell by their effort that they were frantically trying to reach the bank, but the current held the craft fast in an endless downstream spin. They floated by, spinning so fast I don't think they saw me. It must have been like an amusement park ride for them because they laughed all the way downstream and out of sight.

McKenzie boats are used to fish water that is otherwise inaccessible by foot, to float through private property that is closed to the public, or to ply angling techniques on waters that are just too big to wade and fish efficiently. They are highly maneuverable and comfortingly stable on even the most turbulent water. They can be a lot of fun, and a great deal of water can be covered in a day. But one only gets a few casts or drifts of the fly in any given hole, run or riffle. Despite the oarsman's skills it is difficult to keep the craft still long enough for a fly caster to work a spot properly. I don't like them much for that reason alone, but there are others as well. The process of setting up is time consuming, considering a vehicle shuttle with the boat's trailer is necessary to facilitate the take-out at float's end. And on many stretches of river, especially in Colorado, one cannot get out of the boat on private land. Landowners hold title to the river bed in Colorado and many defend that right vociferously. Arguments bordering on fisticuffs have resulted on many occasions and I have witnessed too many. It tends to distract from the ethereal aspects of the endeavor. Of course, there are those who would rather fight than fish. For myself, the fishing is quite battle enough, thank you.

However, I have deigned to join many a friend in possession of such a craft for a day or days on the river over the years, usually with some resulting episode that I would have missed, had I stayed ashore. Such took place on northern New Mexico's San Juan River.

The "Juan" is a huge tail water fishery emanating from the bottom of Navajo Dam. The dam itself is one of the largest earth structures I have ever seen, and the lake behind it is beyond deep, resulting in the coldest water, next to the Green River in Utah, that I have ever shivered in. It is that constant 45 degree temperature that makes for such an excellent fishery. Trout in the 14 to 17 inch range abound and generally have no compunction about taking a fly. Despite the local guides' insistence that only the #24 Teeny Weenies sold in their shops are the fish's fly of preference, I have caught them on everything from #16 Egg patterns to large Chamois Leeches. It is on this river that the (in) famous San Juan Worm was developed, a fly pattern of dubious repute. When coupled with the Egg Pattern in a dropper style double rig it is fondly referred to as "Spaghetti & Meat Balls". It should not be confused with the pattern combination known as "Ham & Eggs" which in fact is an Egg Pattern coupled with a Prince Nymph. God forbid it should be a Bead Head Prince. That's just taking things a bit too far in my view.

Jack, Joufisch and I set off on a highly anticipated trip to that legendary river with Jack's McKenzie boat in tow. We reached Texas Hole on the San Juan one fine crisp October morning about 7 A.M. Texas Hole is the only place to put in on the tail water, and every guide in that area was there doing the same with two clients each. There must have been 15 or more boats circling in the big eddy when we arrived, with several more waiting in line.

I couldn't find my hat. I can't fish without one even on cloudy days. And my dermatologist insists that I wear it. Too many basal cell carcinomas have been removed from my head and face to ignore him. In fact I have accused him of taking more chunks out me than are really necessary. I swear he is cloning me and that somewhere in the dim recesses of his laboratory is a partially constructed doppelganger that he intends to train as his assistant.

I cursed about it, which got Joufisch's attention and he rummaged through his vehicle, producing a spanking new ball cap. It was a cap with the county sheriff's logo where he was employed as a deputy. He wore a corduroy version with the same seven pointed star emblazoned on the fore crown. The last time a I borrowed one of those from him, I walked into a diner where sat a shift of cops on dinner break. I almost had to talk to them. That day I had no choice and figured I wasn't going to see any cops. It was that, or risk another contribution to my doppelganger.

We waited patiently to launch and join the flotilla of boats making a slow circle in the big eddy. The guides let their clients cast while drifting through the big eddy, before heading downstream. One after the other in the order they put in, the boats peeled off for the day's float. There seemed etiquette to the process. We had made only a portion of the loop when Joufisch stood in the bow to make a cast, with Jack at the oars. His first back cast to load the rod hooked the large black Stetson of a guide on the center thwart of the boat behind us. If not for the consummate oarsman ship possessed by Jack, the hat would have been in the drink. A collective gasp ran through the fleet while the guide unhooked himself from Jou's line and angrily tossed it back in our direction. We did not make any friends that morning. I felt like one of those catalog fisherman displayed serenely in the pages of LL Bean, the kind who look good and are photographically bathed in the light of utter civility, yet are clueless.

"Let's get downriver." I whispered in Jack's ear from the stern thwart.

He dipped an oar in the water and with one powerful stroke did an abrupt about face in the eddy and we broke for the current—completely out of turn and again in direct contradiction to the river's unspoken etiquette. I couldn't get enough distance from them.

We fished that morning ahead of the numerous boats full of guided anglers, until we stopped, beaching ourselves on a wet gravel bar, to work a braided section of the river where numerous wade fishermen were scattered along its length. By the time we had covered those areas free of other waders, the fleet appeared upriver and I hastened my companions to board. We shoved off without delay, as none cared for a second encounter. It is important to note that along the San Juan, signs declaring the mandatory use of life vests are well posted. You can't be on the river without noticing them. And although Jack and I wore the cumbersome safety devices, Joufisch refused. He sat on his, claiming it was good enough.

"The signs don't say you have to wear the damn things. It just says required," he irrationally insisted.

We were still ahead of the flotilla when we came upon a truly enticing set of breaks and drops on the lower end of the river, which was separated by a large dry gravel bar. It was just too damned inviting to ignore. Frankly, the fishing had been slow all the way down the river, even at the upper braid section where riffles and holes are plentiful. We beached the boat on the bar and began working the breaks and runs below the drop. I took a minute to change flies while Jack and Joufisch began to cast into the tail of the run. I put on a Wet Caddis emerger with an A.P.M. dropper. I weighted the rig with enough split shot to ensure a good depth during the drift. The first cast brought immediate results. I was rewarded for my patience with a nice rainbow. He took the Midge Dropper with the force of a big dog chasing the mailman and reaching the end of its tether. Jack and Joufisch, of course, inquired as to my bait and I handed each an A.P.M. Midge. We fished the area, catching and releasing some very decent fish for a good hour before the flotilla caught up.

When they did, we were greeted with the same disdainful looks that had been cast upon us earlier that morning. I could almost smell the animosity in the air. Each boat in turn ran the break, either left or right of our position on the bar, with the sole and obvious purpose of disturbing or inhibiting our ability to work the water. We stood our ground while they passed, scowling. It was clear the guides had intended to fish it. The caps prevented altercation, if only verbal, and did nothing to put us in good stead with the local piscatorial entrepreneurs. We let them pass without comment or acknowledgement, and continued productively to ply the waters around the little bar.

After another half an hour of good fishing, and with the flotilla well out of sight, we shoved off downstream. As we approached the upper of two takeouts, the flotilla was lined up against the bank to trailer out, dirty looks seasoned with an uncomfortable vibe clouded the air. I was glad to float to the lower takeout. Taking out with the irritated guides who seemed to really dislike us was far less desirable than floating an extra hour and half, even if the fishing was slow on that lower section. They let us pass with dirty looks and head shakes.

With them off the river and a pleasant float ahead, we relaxed a little more. About forty-five minutes later we rounded a bend in the river. There I noticed a man standing at the river's edge waving furiously for us to pull over.

"Hey pull in here," he demanded, once within earshot.

He was a State Park Ranger. From his neck dangled a large pair of binoculars—really large.

"Where the hell did he come from?" Jack griped.

The road was some six hundred yards uphill on his side. Between him and the road was a forest of Scrub Oak—the kind that pokes and scratches any who pass through it. He had bushwhacked all the way to the river. I could tell that he was pissed.

"Hey, pull that boat in here now!" he demanded forcefully again.

Jack did and that's when the grilling started. First he wanted to know if Jack was a guide and if he had a license and permit for the river. Jack assured him that we were a private party of friends and that the boat belonged to him. Then he wanted to see our fishing licenses, which we produced. Then he railed Joufisch for not wearing his vest.

"You guys should know better, being on the job," he scolded, referring to our caps while Jou stood vest-less at attention in the bow during the entire castigation.

"I've got mine on," I said hooking my thumbs in the arm holes like a proud new father boasting of his first child's birth.

"Me too," Jack said with same exaggerated gesture.

"I should write you guys up and impound your boat. And I would if you weren't on the job. You!" He said pointing an accusatory digit directly at Jou, "should know better. Now get out of here. And get off this river. If I see you below that lower takeout, you're gonna' see the judge."

Through the entire scolding Joufisch could only stand in the bow, stiffer than a bait casting rod, responding to each castigation, with "Yes sir, and thank you officer".

He put his vest on between "yes sirs". As we drifted away the guy looked up the hill at the climb he had before him and then back at us with a wave of disgust. He was crestfallen at the prospect of making the climb without the satisfaction of citing us.

"I'd say Ranger Charlie was someone's brother or brother in-law or some kind of relative and I'll bet my rod that one of those guides called that in—probably the guy in the black Stetson," Jack allowed from the center thwart as the river drifted us from the ranger's view.

"Speaking of hats, I'm gonna' want that back, Cahill. I told ya' these things work."

I didn't give it back, and claimed it as payment for putting me through a day of hell with the locals. It hangs collecting dust in my closet. I refuse to wear the damn thing.

The flotilla on the San Juan

# Drift 13

# Bubba's Chub

One unfortunate side effect of McKenzie boat floating is that your companions are no further than a boat length away. Invariably, proximity breeds familiarity and chatter becomes incessant, progressing to the point of distraction. On top of that, each mate is subject to the outright buffoonery of the others. A rocking boat is fertile loam for mishap of at least a comical nature. I have the scars to prove the number of times I've been hit with an oar or lead weight, knocked down, stepped on or flat-out snagged by the careless back cast of everybody. Sitting in the stern has some drawbacks, but I don't think being tallied as part of the catch should be one of them. And then there is the inevitable cast over. It never fails to amaze me when the other angler tangles his line over mine, and I am equally mortified if mine is the offender—oh well, such are the vagaries of close-proximity fishing.

Yet, I have and suppose I will continue to let my guard down when asked to join a float. When Jack called early one Sunday morning to invite me along with himself and Bubba on the Colorado between

New Castle and Silt, Colorado; I did just that. It's not the best section of the Colorado to float, nor the wildest; in fact it's one of the easiest. But there are far fewer anglers and boaters on it in October, and I have rarely failed to catch at least one 3 to 5 pounder whenever I have fished it. On such occasions, for the most part, we have had the river entirely to ourselves. It can be a grand day, with lunch alfresco.

The perspective from the boat is entirely different, and can afford the opportunity to glide right up to wildlife that would be spooked by the shore wader. Deer, Elk, Fox, Marmot, Weasels and Pine Martens are not uncommon to sight, and a myriad of water fowl seem ubiquitous. We came upon a bevy of Bonaparte's Gulls working a hatch just above the water's surface on this very stretch only some years before. The sighting was unusual, for they are not indigenous to the Colorado basin. They stayed right alongside the boat for a good part of the day. A storm front must have blown them in. I had to look them up in Sibley's Guide when I got home. I couldn't believe it, but that's what they were. And just to ice the cake, I have seen eagles and osprey fishing. Of course, this has a damping effect on the fishing, but poor fishing is pittance a fee to remit for the pleasure of watching such skilled anglers ply their trade.

We shoved off on a beautiful fall morning. I had known Bubba for twenty-odd years but this was the first time we had fished together. He loaded a spinning rod and a fly rod in the boat. Jack had told stories about him. So I was on my guard for something interesting to occur. The cottonwoods along the river were in the waxy yellow stage that makes them appear to contain an inner light. I could barely keep my mind on fishing and spent a good part of the day just looking. Only a few hundred yards downstream from the launch, the chatter began. Bubba looked up from his rigging task and swiveled in the front seat to face us. I knew something was coming.

"How long do you think we'll be out here?" he asked.

"I don't know. Depends on the fishing and how many stops we make," Jack allowed as he dipped and stroked an oar to avoid a large submerged rock. "Why?" he asked prodding Bubba.

"Well, I got a date tonight and I need to be back by six or so."

Although I'd seen him frequently in the course of having a life, I couldn't remember the last time I saw him with a lady.

"You do?" Jack congratulated. "Well who is it? Is she a nice girl? Where did you meet her?"-a flurry of interrogatories.

"Oh, she's a real nice girl," Bubba boasted. "Real pretty and smart and all. But, I don't know. We're just going out for dinner and a movie."

"What do you mean, you don't know?" Jack pushed for more.

"Well, she's got a bottom the size of a $20 pizza." He looked up from his rigging and grinned, eyebrows raised over an impish twinkle.

In the bow, Bubba chuckled to himself and worked the water a with spinning outfit. His fly rod leaned against the bow compartment like an antenna. The long spin casts, loudly plunked well astern, were taking their toll on my tolerance. He was effectively eating up more than half the available water by virtue of his method. I had to fish on the port forequarter no matter where the boat was in relation to the bank or current. He just kept casting and cranking down the larboard quarter. After an hour or so of this unrelenting plunk and retrieve, he stopped to remove the tablespoon-sized spinner he'd been throwing. While he fussed with his rig, I took advantage of the opportunity to work the water on the seam of the main current and the slack water. Jack, ever the consummate guide, kept the boat at just the right position for an easy drift. I caught several good fish for my efforts and because of Jack's.

I noticed Bubba rummaging through his large metal tackle box that was perched on the forward compartment deck of the bow.

"What the hell are you doing up there Bubba?" I groused over Jack's head

"I'm looking for my syringe." He threw a sheepish glance over his shoulder at me

"Your what?"

"My syringe," he sniped.

Jack turned to me in the stern, his face painted with disbelief. I shrugged—as if to say a syringe? On a fly fishing trip? And who even owns a syringe? My doctor was all I could think of.

"Here it is." Bubba said. His voice crackled with the timbre of relief. Then he held up the new rig, a big bait hook with a large open sproat. The hook was threaded with a thick, meaty night crawler. A foot above the hook and worm, a lead dropper swung from a 3-way swivel. The chunk of lead was big—way too big. The Colorado is deep and fast, but it ain't that deep or fast. In the other hand he held the syringe. Drawing the plunger back, thus filling the tube with air, he stuck the bent needle into the wriggling worm.

"If ya' inject them with a little air they're more buoyant and give better action underwater. This way the worm doesn't wrap around the hook."

He cast it. It was a basic chuck and duck technique. He did the chucking and we did the ducking. It made a whizzing noise when it passed me, hitting the water like a thrown rock. I almost felt it through the boat with my feet. It sounded like the thud skulls make when knocked together, so the fish knew we were there. I reeled in and let him continue, content to watch the scenery and daydream. I didn't really care where he cast or what he threw. I was good with it all. Eventually he snagged something on the river bottom. He thought it was a fish, of course, and set the hook. I knew it wasn't by the rod. It bowed terribly and I hoped it would snap. Then he would be forced to pick up the fly rod. It didn't.

He begged Jack to swing the boat around and get upstream of the snag, claiming it was his only hook. I said a quick parochial chant under my breath for the line to snap. The 12 lb. test didn't heed my supplication, and the boat almost swung around of the line's accord before Jack could stroke an oar. The water was placid and Jack easily made enough upstream headway for Bubba to get his rod tip above the snag. Bubba jerked with authority several times and the snag released its grasp. It careened wildly towards us. The hook was dangerous enough, but that enormous sinker was a deadly projectile. I snickered a little when it hit him square in the chest. Undaunted, he continued, stopping only occasionally to inflate the worm.

After a few more miles and several more snagging incidents, even Jack was irritated, and he hadn't fished, only rowed. He wanted out of the boat and said so. He swung the craft onto a lightly submerged bar a few miles above the take out. There he dropped anchor and got out to fish a deep channel against the bank. A large moraine bluff loomed over the channel's course and the sun, already low in the October sky, cast a good cover shadow on the water.

While Jack fished with his back to the boat, Bubba continued to work his lead and worm rig in the main channel just off the bow. I had just enough water on Jack's side of the gravel bar, at the head of his channel, to make some short drift casts from the stern. Deciding to change flies, I took the rear seat and swiveled to the bow. Bubba had actually hooked a fish. He played it for a bit and then hauled a large Chub into the boat. I commented on the size and advised him that he might want to release the fish as it was a protected species. While the big Chub flopped on the deck, he rummaged his tackle box again and produced an enormous pair of needle nose pliers. Grabbing the fish behind the gills, he reached down its gullet with them to remove the deeply embedded hook.

"Man, that's way down there," he said, as he mercilessly probed the fish.

"Just cut the line and let the fish go, Bubba. The hook will rust out in no time. If you keep jabbing it like that, you'll probably kill it." I cautioned.

I turned my back and tried my luck in the little channel head again, leaving him to his dilemma and the fish to its plight. I really didn't care to watch. Behind me I could hear the familiar clatter of his rummaging. I kept fishing, trying to force myself not to look. Finally, I couldn't stand it anymore and had to take a peek. Bubba held up the line with the fish head hanging above his. He squinted up the fish's neck, probing with the long needle nose.

"There!" he said, pulling the hook out from the rough hewn end. He held the hook and worm in the jaws of the pliers and let the fish head slide down his line. Then, and only then, he cut the line at the hook eye and pulled it through the head. The fish head fell to the deck next to the rest of the carcass.

"Got it!" Bubba bragged, proudly displaying the saved hook securely in the jaws of the pliers. He began to re-rig and ignored the carcass and gore. Blood was everywhere. The fish head fluttered its gills, not knowing death had come. In its last dying gasp, Jack returned to the gunwale from his little side fish. When he saw the carnage, he turned ashen and somber.

"Jesus Bubba! What the hell are you doing?" He gasped.

"Oh, I had to get that hook out—it's my only one. Don't worry, it's not a trout."

"No, but it's a Chub and you can't kill those," Jack scolded. He grabbed the two pieces and flung them as far up over the bluff as he could.

"At least something can make use of it."

Using a bail bucket, he washed the blood from where it speckled our craft, diluting it to the bottom. Then he made us pull the fully loaded boat onto shore and drain the evidence out the stern plugs before he would shove off. With the shame of murder erased, Jack rowed the last few miles downstream, like a posse with a noose was behind us. He was sullen and paranoid, convinced that someone had seen the entire episode and was on the phone right then, calling the Chub Police. A previous and unfortunate infraction, resulting in extremely short-term incarceration and a fine, drove his effort. He rowed so furiously that all I could do was drag the fly behind in the current. Bubba fished the whole way. Jack rowed fast enough to keep him from snagging. While he fished, Bubba groused about the time.

We covered the distance quickly, loaded the boat onto the waiting trailer, and made haste for the other truck upstream (my truck), before the Chub Police could arrive. Even with Jack's all-out rowing effort, the float took a little longer than Bubba had allowed. He was agitated during the drive back upstream. He calmed down a little bit when we reached the parking spot in New Castle. He must have said something to Jack, because when I got out to unload my gear from the boat, I barely had time enough to grab it and say thanks before they tore off, boat wagging behind them.

Bubba was late. I guess he didn't want that pizza to get cold. Nobody likes a big cold pizza; not at least, until breakfast.

Erasing the evidence of the murdered Chub

# Drift 14

# Naps

While in high school, I learned the value of a nap when I became a late night short order cook for a chain of popular restaurants. With a five day a week schedule of school and work, few hours were available for sleep. Young bodies can endure a lot. I got through with naps in last period study hall after my work was done. On the few week days that I had only school to deal with, I came straight home and took a nap. I habitually lay under an antique deacon's bench that adorned the living room in every house we resided. I did this so that my little brothers couldn't mess with me, and because it was close to the door Jack entered. When he arrived, I could jump up real quick to pretend I wasn't napping. I'm sure he knew. The bench resides in my living room now. I no longer have the svelte to fit under it, so I've taken to napping on it. The nap got me through back then. They continued to sustain me through the grueling rigors of college, while I sold ladies' shoes in a department store to fund my education. I could doze standing up at my station back then. I have snapped awake to the ghastly view of more bunions and hammer toes than any man should know about.

"Young man, do you have this in a size six?" they'd croak, wiggling a stocking clad painted toenail foot, with at least some distressed quality to it, maybe one toe pointing straight up, a horrifying apparition to a young man in his full vigor. Of course, I knew six meant nine. Armed with a pair of each I knelt, taking the foot with the offending digit in my hand.

I also worked once for a man who owned a small ranch, and took naps after lunch. I built a new barn for him over the course of a summer between snoozes. I've napped in vehicles, under bridges, in fire towers, on offshore drilling platforms under the steady thrumming of a Cummins diesel, and in boulder fields. Naps have always been a source of second wind for me. It is small wonder that naps and fishing go together. It's a universal practice. Endless depictions of fishermen, clad in a straw hat, overalls, with bare feet, sleeping against a stately tree trunk on the edge of some water, while holding a cane pole with a bobber rippling the surface, decorate our culture.

And so of course I, too, have napped during the fishing day. Usually during the slow period of the day when the fish become uncooperative and the stress of travel takes its toll. The weather must be at least clement. Jack hates it when I nap. He usually fishes close by while I doze, fettered by the fear that something might eat me and frustrated by the chain of babysitting, which prevents him from plying the more enticing water just beyond those links' reach. I believe he hangs about until I wake because he dreads the prospect of dragging my half-eaten carcass back to the truck. Should he care to catch forty winks, well then, it doesn't matter if I get eaten.

We put in one sunny April morning from the upper access on the Rio Grande lease at South Fork, Colorado with eight-foot pontoon boats. The river was low but the little boats drew only inches, and we easily glided over many a low section that would otherwise require portage, and prevented other boats from floating the river. We had the entire lease to ourselves early in the season, another good reason to take a fishing trip in early April. The conditions for a post-lunch nap were perfect and nagging.

We spent the morning leisurely floating the river and beaching our small craft at any likely spot. Our results were limited. The Rio Grande was still suffering from the onslaught of Whirling Disease, but we knew that before we put in, so disappointment was not an issue. Any negative thoughts were instantly assuaged by the our delightful bob along a river made famous by many a Hollywood western, while under the brilliant blue that only Colorado skies can achieve, all without another soul in sight. It was bucolically soothing when laid atop the film of cabin fever.

As midday came upon us, the hefty breakfast we had indulged in was spent by the repetitive launching, beaching, and wading. The hollow of hunger and heavy lids drove our search for a likely spot to eat and rest. We found it right away and beached our little boats in a small eddy adjacent to a grassy point that jutted into the current and was well carpeted with a thick mat of last year's growth, made all the denser by the deer who had bedded there over the course of the winter. Tender shoots of new green reached for the sunlight through it. It was perfect for our purpose. Lunch tasted all the better for it. With full bellies and eyelids drooping, we rolled and fluffed our vests into pillows, making sure that the sharp corners of fly boxes and such did not protrude into ear or nape. I lay on my back and wiggled down into the soft brown turf staring into the blue, and then pulled my Rooster Cogburn over my brow. I'm not sure about Jack, but I fell away like a sated baby. I woke to a semi-conscious state several times to hear Jack snoring over the gurgle of the current, and dozed right back into the one-eyed half sleep that naps are.

I think what finally roused me was the silence and the cool gust of spring wind falling off the La Garitas. I shivered a little despite the caress of the April sun. I stood to stretch and put my gear together when I noticed one of the boats was gone. My first thought was—"Shit! How far has that gone?" The prospect of searching the river to Del Norte or beyond was daunting to say the least. Then I noticed that Jack was gone also. I felt better about the boat. My relief was quickly overcome by a serious miff at Jack for leaving me to be eaten. After all, this was serious mountain lion country, not to mention the prevalence of lesser carnivores like coyotes. I'd been stalked by both before with my wits and weapons fully about me. The thought of lying asleep with neither in my possession sent a cold chill from my tailbone to my neck. I could have been stepped on by a cow. And the other things a cow could have done to me seemed even less desirable. Now I was getting pissed that he'd left me. I objected aloud to his very existence.

I jumped in my boat and rowed hard and fast to overtake him, cursing his being with each power stroke of the oars. The rowing and cursing drained my anger and when I finally caught up to him several miles downstream it had left me. He stood on the upper edge of a long riffle.

"'Bout time you got up," was all he said.

I ignored him and floated through his drift, rowing and splashing my oar blades to spook any fish that might be holding there-so much for fly fishing etiquette, at least between friends.

One of the most unnerving naps I have taken was on the McCloud River in northern California under the shadow of Mount Shasta. Once again I found myself on some river right after the Labor Day holiday, with no other people in sight. I had traveled some 12 hours by air, (most of it waiting for connecting flights), from Grand Junction, Colorado to Sacramento, California where Jack picked me up late that afternoon. We drove another few hours to the headwaters of the Trinity River to fish for King Salmon and Steelhead below Trinity Dam, upstream of Weaverville. I caught several nice Kings while there and Jack got skunked despite the steelhead breaching about him. I think it was karmic payback for leaving me asleep on the Rio Grande that previous spring. Or, maybe he just wasn't holding his lips right. It was his first time after either species. It was not mine.

The afternoon of the second day found us in lawn chairs at a remote put-in on the middle Trinity. The day had turned hot and the fishing slow. The best way to pass such a period is to nap, and we did so with rods rigged and leaning against the chair arm, just in case the splash of migrating fish happened to disturb our rest. It did not. Lawn chair naps are good.

By the third day we had our fill of the icy water that issues from the bottom of Trinity Dam, and made our way toward the McCloud on the eastern slopes of Mount Shasta below the century-old company logging town of McCloud. The McCloud is a Nature Conservancy river piercing the heart of Shasta-Trinity National Forest. Only eight miles of the river are open to fishing and that is limited to ten fishermen per day. Access is controlled by a reservation and walk-up quota. There are five tags for each hanging on a board at the conservator's cabin where the open water begins. Fishermen must walk in the mile and a half from the parking lot to the cabin. A sign at the trail head instructs the fisherman or hiker to carry a piece of firewood from the large pile under it. The conservators live there year round. The wood is the fuel by which they cook and heat their remote home. We loaded ourselves with several pieces each.

At the cabin the fisherman (or hiker) must take one of the ten numbered tags hanging on the sign-in board next to the conservator's cabin in accordance with one's status. If the five walk-up tags are gone and one does not have a reservation, he may not fish or even walk the river trail. This day we were delighted to see that all the tags remained on the board. We took two walk-ups from the board and hung them by their shower curtain hooks to our vests. As we signed in, the conservator came out to greet us and thanked us for bringing some extra wood beyond the required piece per man.

While Jack chatted with the conservator, I took one of the single sheet maps of the river from its display box next to the tag board. I listened politely as the conservator gave us the required introductory talk about the Conservancy. It was during the spiel that I looked the map over and noticed some of the holes on the river had names with the word "Rattlesnake" in them. My heart raced and then sank. The old angst of my youth draped itself over me like a cold, wet blanket. A little shiver came over me.

"Are rattlers about on the river?" I interrupted.

"Yes," the conservator answered, then thanked us again and returned to the cabin. I wanted to leave right then. Jack must have smelled the discomfort on me or at least read the contorted knit of my brow. "What the hell's wrong with you?"

"I don't like snakes—at all," I said, handing him the map and pointing to a hole named "Rattlesnake Pit".

"Well, we're here; might as well fish it," he said.

"Yeah but you didn't tell me about the snakes and I don't have a bite kit or a pistol," I complained. "Let's go," he said and turned down the river trail.

I followed, trying not to touch the ground as I walked. Even my great fear of rattlesnakes could not diminish the overwhelming beauty of the place. It was almost primeval. It seemed, like so few places do, to be as it had always been. Towering Douglas firs shaded the trail and the ground was covered with Hemlock and Ferns of many varieties. Where large Douglas firs had fallen across the trail, a half round notch had been neatly sawed from the fallen giant and split in two. The quarters lay on either side of the massive trunk, thus providing the walker with a step on each side to cross the huge timber. These cuts were the only sign that any human had been there before us.

The river itself was a deep, powerful waterway. Not wider than any other western river I have fished, but the holes were far deeper and large pickup truck size boulders littered its course. The color was a green I had not seen before, perhaps a mirror image of the forest through which it ran. It was a treacherous wade, even where wade-able. Getting a drift was difficult at best. Each hole was subject to a series of trial and error casts and mends, until the desired drift could be attained, if at all. Fishing it was not easy. The specter of rattlesnakes loomed with every step and was a constant distraction for me. Yet our diligence was rewarded with several large fish each. The morning passed without sight of a snake, but even so, choosing a lunch spot was a matter of great distress to me. We found a sweet little clearing on the water's edge. It was moss-covered and gently sloped towards the river. Several small boulders dotted it. It looked inviting; nonetheless, I spent a good bit of time poking the underbrush around it with the tip of my poor, abused fly rod, just to be sure.

Of course lunch was followed by a nap, but not before I poked around one more time with my fly rod. Skittishly, I settled down on the soft moss carpet and tucked my rolled vest and pack under my head. I left the waterproof camera that I always carry on a strap around my neck, resting on my chest. A faint snore rattled from the other side of the small boulder that separated our heads and shoulders. I looked down the length of my body to see the river flowing just beyond our four feet shod in felt-soled boots, toes pointing toward the sky. It was an uneasy snooze.

We spent the afternoon fishing our way back up the trail. It was a grueling day. On the ride back to McCloud, we noticed a mileage sign informing the reader 9 miles remained to the town. Two miles down the road, the next sign declared it was now 11 miles to the town. We got a good chuckle out of it after realizing we WERE headed in the right direction. We spent that night in the restored McCloud Hotel in the town that bears its name. No phones, no TV, the rooms were furnished in the décor of those times. It was the best night's rest I have ever had on the road.

When I returned home and had the pictures from the trip developed, I found a shot of those two pairs of wading boots, sticking straight up, with the McCloud River in the background. I really don't know how that happened.

In August many summers ago, after he retired, I took Jack to a little reservoir on the upper south fork of the Frying Pan to belly boat. He had never used one before and relished the opportunity. The place is called Chapman Reservoir and was built during the depression by the CCC. It's a fine little ten acre impoundment and can have some good fishing. Mostly it is a put and take fishery. There is no boat ramp and motorized craft are prohibited.

It took forever to get the boats inflated and Jack dressed, rigged and into one of them. We fished from the center in towards the shore with little luck, finally becoming separated. I worked my way against a steady breeze, toward the deeper water by the dam. After about an hour, I spun the boat around to see Jack way at the other end of the lake in the reeds. I thought that was kind of a stupid place to fish. The water at that end of the little lake was only six or eight inches deep and choked with reeds and water grasses. I didn't give it much more thought and continued to work my way back and forth across the front of the dam. I even changed my reel spool out to a sinking line and began to troll the deep water, confident that I could connect with a big lunker who had somehow managed to survive the put and take cycle. It happens!

On one of my about-face moves to make another pass along the dam, I noticed out of the corner of my eye that Jack had not moved from the shallow reedy end of the lake. On second look, I realized that his head was lolled over onto his chest. Jack was an older gentleman in his late 60's by then, and I feared the worst, that he'd had a heart attack and drifted with the wind to the other end.

I reeled in and began to kick paddle with my fins as hard and fast as I could. Thank God the wind was with me. It took me a while to get down there to him, and when I entered that shallow reedy end I couldn't get a good kick with my fins because there just wasn't enough water under me. I had to push myself along with the heels of my wading boots. Finally, after stirring up enough mud to make bricks, I bumped against Jack's belly boat. He came instantly awake.

"Damn! You scared the hell out me." He complained.

"What the hell, Jack? I thought you were dead the way your head was hanging over." I told him.

"No, I was just napping. This damn thing is so comfortable it put me to sleep. How long was I out?"

# Drift 15

# New Guy
# (How Stumpy Got His Name)

Near about every spring for the last twenty or so years, I have taken a fishing trip. After spending five to six months in the snow of the Rockies it's hard not to think of anything but warmer weather and shucking off the debilitating effects of cabin fever. Usually about the middle of January I can't stand it anymore and pull out the old fly tying kit. At least I can gain some relief by tying flies for a few weekends while sitting in front of my greenhouse TV, listening to old westerns. I am a dyed in the wool John Wayne fan, but any old western will do for background distraction from the tedium of fly tying. Although I've seen them all dozens of times, they lend a certain comfort and ease to the task. I can look up from my crouch over the vise and refocus my eyes on someone being shot or punched. Sometimes I have to settle for a "007" marathon, which seems to run every year about that time, but that's OK, for I get the same punches and shootings. To me, it's like having the stereo on while housecleaning or performing some other obsequious task. I consider fly tying to be in that category, but I have to do it if I want to fish.

Eventually I have a few hundred tied up and arranged in those big flat plastic compartmentalized Plano boxes, enough to see me and Jack through the year, dry flies notwithstanding. He doesn't tie. Once the task is completed it's usually about time for the weather to change enough to warrant being on the river. By then I've seen and heard enough of the Duke and Bond to last me until the next midwinter bout with cabin fever.

It's then that I take a trip to somewhere in the state where the weather and the water are a little warmer, and that usually (always) means the Lower Gunnison, Lake Fork, Rio Grande and Conejos Rivers. It's my starter trip for the year. I hardly ever miss it. Plus, it eats up a good week, soothing my soul and preventing me from perpetrating some regrettable act, caused by the distemper of my funk.

I set off in the second week of March with Jack and a New Guy, with whom we had never before fished. We left late one afternoon bound for the Rio Grande at the town of South Fork, Colorado. Our late start prevented the customary afternoon stop to fish the Lake Fork of the Gunnison. Instead we took an alternate route through Gunnison, Colorado then up Cochetopa Creek, over North Pass, and down into the tiny ranching community of Saguache. It's pronounced "Sa-watch" but we say "Sagooche". Somebody mispronounced it one trip and the name stuck. In "Sagooche," New Guy was stopped by the local constabulary for a speed violation. I had let him take over driving my truck somewhere around Los Pinos Creek where it passes through the Coleman Ranch, well above the little town. This unplanned stop ate up a little time while New Guy received his ticket, so we took a short cut I know from "Sagooche" to Del Norte, skirting the feet of the LaGarita Mountains. I drove. Despite the short cut we arrived in South Fork a little late.

Fishing day dawned cold and overcast, but we didn't let that dissuade us from getting on the river. We possessed the gear to spend the day in the foulest of conditions. We set off early that morning for the lower bridge on the DOW easement just east of town.

The easement along U.S. 160 is a marvelous section of river. It's about ten or so miles long and can be accessed at three points where county roads cross the river. As long as one enters the lease from the public access point he can walk freely along the river bank, even though it is well off the main highway and surrounded by private land. During the spring and after Labor Day, there isn't a soul on it. Lately I have taken to floating it in my one man pontoon boat; I get a shuttle upstream from the great folks at the Rainbow Grocery. But on this day we walked.

The morning started with intermittent snow flurries, changing to light rain as the day warmed slightly. Fishing was slow because the Rio Grande, like many western rivers, was suffering from the height of whirling disease. It's a parasite that affects rainbows in the 11 to 14 inch range. The bug causes a deformation of cartilage which literally bends the fish, causing it to swim in circles, hence the name whirling disease. They can't feed in the latter stages and die. Most of our rivers have been affected to some degree, and many to a great degree. In those places where the disease has taken hold, the once prolific and predominant Rainbows are replaced by Brown Trout in a sort of natural selection process. Browns don't seem to be affected.

So we weren't surprised by the slow fishing. We were really more interested in getting loose from the daily grind. Just to be able to walk along a river without two or three feet of snow on its banks was enough. But I was surprised to catch my first ever Rio Grande Cutthroat. It was a nice healthy fish about fourteen inches big. We made about three miles walking and fishing upriver before the sun broke through and the day warmed to pleasant. We came upon a spot where a pair of snapped-off cottonwood trunks stood right on the edge of the river bank over a deep and fast channel. The trunks were about 15 to 20 feet in height and had grown from the same root system. They were about 18 to 20 inches in diameter and stood like a "V" for victory sign. The downstream trunk was the terminus end of a barbed wire line running deep into a rancher's pasture. By the rules of access we were not allowed into that field; 20 feet above the high water mark is all we had to work with, and there was too much brush along the line of wire within that 20 feet to allow us any easy means of passage.

Fly fishermen tend to avoid barbed wire. We're like cattle that way. There are just too many things that can get ruined by it. Waders can be punctured, shirts and vests easily torn, hats are just about always knocked off while scooting under it, and anything dangling from a vest is easily snatched by the stuff. Even if another man is there to separate the strands, there is always some problem, and older guys like us really don't like crawling under things with all that gear on. It's too hard to get up on our feet again. To make life a little easier, we are always looking for a way around barbed wire. And this wire ended at the downstream trunk. If we stepped through the "V" created by the two broken cottonwoods, we could easily circumvent the nasty bite of its teeth, decorated with tufts of cattle hair.

Jack took the lead and stepped into the V. As he passed through, the trunk with the wire wiggled.

"Watch that trunk, you guys it's kind of loose." He warned.

New Guy went through next and the trunk wiggled again. I stepped up and my day pack bumped the unfettered trunk, sending me forward with my full weight on the loose and wired one. It wiggled tenuously but I made it through without incident. I made a mental note to find another way through the fence wire on the way back.

We continued to fish for a bit with the same limited success for another half mile, when it was unanimously agreed to stop for lunch. There in the soft, brown grass of last year's growth we nestled down to eat and shoot the breeze. There were lots of stories, gripes, bitches, and belly laughs to season our meal. Eventually we removed our vests and rolled them into pillows for a short nap, as always after a good stuffing in the open air. The newly arrived sun had dried the grass and its warmth did little to prevent our doze. The inclement morning seemed a distant inconvenience.

I woke to the rattle of Jack's snore and hauled myself to my feet.

"Hey! Get up you slugs. It's getting late and we have a good three miles back to the truck. Come on!" I prodded.

They groaned and grunted themselves upright, complaining all the while that I hadn't baked enough toll house cookies for the trip and how they could use a couple more for the walk back. After a few more minutes of complaining about stiffening joints and sweaty waders, we managed to shake the stupid that follows any nap and began to gather ourselves for the trek back downriver. About halfway to the broken and teetering cottonwood sentinels we entered a little copse of small evergreen trees growing along the trail. New Guy stopped dead in his tracks.

"Shit, crap, goddamn it!" He spewed

"What?" Jack asked.

"I left my vest back at the lunch spot," New Guy admitted.

"See ya' down river," I teased. Jack stood in silence with a big mule eatin' briars grin on his mug.

"I'm gunna' leave my rod here," New Guy said leaning his brand new 5 weight, which he was trying out for the first time, up against one of the little evergreens.

"We won't be far. I wanna' fish that little side channel below those wiggly cottonwoods we passed on the way up. See ya' down there," I comforted him.

New Guy took off up the trail for the lunch spot, whacking his way through the little willow thicket that encumbered a good part of the trail between the evergreens and there. Jack and I headed downstream to the little side channel. Behind us we could hear the steadily diminishing sounds of New Guy's upriver trek.

"Shit! Crap! God Damn It!" And then faintly, "Son of a bitch!"

We walked about 20 yards into the evergreen copse to find an old kids' spinning rig on the trail. It had one of those push button, closed spool reels on it and was still rigged with a bobber and hook. I don't know how we missed it on the way up. I guess we were actually on the river at that point. Jack picked it up with the glint of mischief in his eye.

"Let's go back and change this out for his fly rod," he chortled.

"Yes!" I agreed.

This is what buddies do to each other. And messing with the New Guy was part and parcel to his first trip with us. If your new buddies are willing to take time from their personal agendas to mess with you, it was the highest compliment that can be paid-acceptance. We have all come to expect it over the years. As a perpetrator and a victim, I can say that either role is frosted with equal sweetness.

Jack and I quickly made our way back to the little evergreen copse where New Guy's rod rested against a short little spruce. We made the exchange. Then we and the new fly rod hid a few yards away behind a shock of elders with some tall brown grass to lie in thus covering our peep from New Guy. We could barely contain ourselves and the air was full of giggles and shushes. We gained control of our glee when we heard him bushwhacking his way back through the willow thicket. He was moving fast. The whip-like crack of willow limbs thwacking his Goretex waders grew steadily louder as he hustled to catch up to us. So did his expletives. Jack let out a little snort trying to contain himself. I elbowed his ribs as I lay peering through the grass and elder trunks.

The jab only exacerbated his containment problem and he damn near gave us away. I shushed him again.

"Shut up. This is gonna' be good," I whispered over his little snorts.

New Guy emerged from the willow thicket at full throttle. He walked to the little evergreen which held the funky kids' rod. He stopped short of the little tree, staring at it. He cocked his head like a dog listening for something in the wind, and then did a 360 to survey the little copse. Then he back-tracked to the edge of the willow thicket, and retraced his steps to the little tree holding the rod. He walked all the way around it, looking intently from side to side. When he completed the circle he stopped dead in front of the kids' rod and picked it up. Turning it over in his hand he inspected it thoroughly, as if the intensity of his gaze would turn it into a 9 foot 5 weight fly rod. He spun again holding the kid rod. Jack and I tried to stifle our delight but he heard us.

"Alright assholes, where's my rod?"

He still hadn't spotted us behind the elder row. We stood with faces cracking from our grins. We all had a good laugh and headed downstream to fish our way back to the truck. Approaching the teetering cottonwood stumps, we separated. Jack and I began to search the fence line for any gap we could squeeze through, and New Guy went for the V between the stumps. I turned back toward the river to look down the fence as New Guy stepped into the crux. I was maybe twenty feet away when he yelled.

The wiggly stump that was the terminus end of the fence line began to fall back towards the river taking New Guy with it. He managed to push off the falling timber, which put him straight down into the fast, waist-deep channel below. His chest and armpits caught the grass-covered loam of the bank. I heard him strike the soft bank with his upper torso. He grunted and looked up at me. Surprise and fright glazed his eyes, though still he managed a faint smile and almost laughed, but the wind was knocked out of him. A little wheeze came out of his mouth as if he were trying to speak.

The 18 foot log fell with its top piercing the swift current. Then the fence line jerked the thick bottom end down across his head and shoulders. I could hear the thud and felt it with my feet. The big tree trunk bounced off him but the current swept the wet end downstream; the barbed wire securely attached to it jerked the thing back down and it trounced him again. This time the log rolled off him and lay with its bottom on the bank and its top in the river, like a spoon upside down in a mug of coffee. It rocked a little back and forth to the rhythm of the current until it settled against a rock or in a hole.

The instant he started to fall, I dropped my rod and sprinted the seven or eight steps to the bank. If a fat boy in waders, boots, vest and pack, huffing his way along is sprinting, then that's what I was doing. I slid up to him face first. It was a major league one, into home plate. Leaves, grass and dirt funneled into the top of my open shirt and jacket. I seized his vest by the lapels just as his knees buckled and he began to lose his tenuous armpit grip on the bank. Digging my elbows into it and using my body as a counterweight gave me enough leverage to keep him half standing. New Guy is a good size boy, and he had the current and a full load of gear in his favor. When his head lolled on his shoulders and his eyes rolled back to white, the sheer dead weight of him began to drag me over the edge. Within a few seconds my elbows were under the bank and I was staring at the water. I yelled for Jack.

"Stay with me!" I commanded New Guy.

I couldn't help but think about that other tree stump and looked over my right shoulder to check it, but all I could see was the blur of Jack rushing in to lend a hand. New Guy came to and got his legs under himself. It was all we could do to drag him up on the chest-high bank. He bitched about us hurting his shoulder. I think he was in shock, because his shoulder was hurt before we grabbed him. We lay on the open, grassy bank regaining our wind, and New Guy his senses. I could see the remaining stump upside down in my view. I wasn't about to lie there waiting for the other shoe to drop. I got to my feet. New Guy lay on his back, with his new 5 weight tight in his fist.

Jack and I grunted him to his feet. Blood trickled down his chin from the hole he'd bit through his tongue when his face was hammered into the ground-twice-and one arm hung limp at his side. We did a slow shuffle with his arms over our shoulders to a cottonwood trunk lying on the ground a few yards inland and well removed from the drop zone of the other shoe. Thinking back, all those cottonwoods on the ground around there might have been a clue. He still held the fly rod when we sat him down on another fallen cottonwood log.

I found a rafting strap in my pack and made a sling for his arm. He walked the three miles out under his own power. He was tough and he could take a joke. Jack and I carried his gear, but he wouldn't let go of that fly rod. We didn't fish on the way back to the truck. He didn't say anything either. At the truck he tried to speak but that bitten tongue was swollen. It was comical hearing him talk. Jack and I laughed, of course, and it pissed him off. We could tell that by his delivery, not the words-they were unintelligible. I offered to take him to the hospital or just home, but he would have none of it. We spent the night in South Fork wining and dining. The guy was amazing.

The next day he relented and allowed us to take him home. On the way we stopped at the river where we had parked the day before. Jack and I dressed in waders for a quick hike up to the tree spot. We hoped to find New Guy's glasses somewhere close by. New Guy slept soundly under the shell of my pickup on a nice thick foam pad. Jack groused the whole way up. We tried to move the tree, but it was far too heavy and we couldn't budge it. As best we could tell, the glasses had fallen in the channel with New Guy. We did find a face print in the soft, loamy bank-clearly defined brow, nose and chin. The soft ground likely saved him a concussion, let alone a fracture. Jack talked about the weight of the tree and what a bad ass New Guy was, all the way back to the truck.

We reckoned during our return leg conversation that if we hadn't taken time to mess with him and the rod, he would have been alone when the tree fell. We agreed that we would have found another way through the wire and not used the V. We were already headed that way before the incident. If not for our dalliance in the copse we surely would have been way down, if not across the river and seen him float by. It was that serious an accident. Funny how those things work out. We each have many such examples of our survival of life thus far. This was one of New Guy's.

On the drive home he slept behind the front seat in the extended cab of my pickup. While he slumbered, Jack and I ate his share of the tollhouse cookies. We didn't go through "Sagooche," but over the Black Mesa instead. Instinctively, he woke when we reached Paonia, about dinner time. We stopped to imbibe and sup at Little's. I always loved that place. The massive log timbers, circular fireplace, and almost private ante rooms were so comforting after a long, hard fish. Little's was a landmark and the food was always wonderful. It was a hard place to leave after a couple of beers and a sumptuous meal. Many times serious discussion took place over who should, rather than who could, drive. The road over McClure Pass is dark and lonely. Deer and elk are always on it. It was during that discussion that I coined his moniker. It was there, bathed in the glow of his survival, under the comfort and ambiance of Little's roof, that he became Stumpy.

Stumpy's Stump

# Drift 16

# There's a lot of waiting when you're a dog

I used to look at those who brought their dogs on the river with some disdain. Usually, the dogs would bark at the other fishermen or disturb the water, or just be a pain if allowed by their masters to roam at will.

I recall one instance while fishing the upper Roaring Fork below Shale Bluffs with Jack. It was early in the year, and snow still covered most of the trail along the river and banks. We were hard-pressed to find a spot that was clear enough to sit comfortably, let alone take a nap after lunch. But we found one on the edge of the trail that faced south and was bare of snow. The previous year's growth was dry. We sat just off the trail with our feet only inches above it. I laid my pack down below us and spread the lunch out on top of it. As we ate and the sun warmed us, a man and his dog came down the trail. It was one of those big, goofy, overly friendly Labradors. I could see that it was vectoring in right on us, and more specifically the lunch at our feet. Standing, I picked up the whole pack with the lunch still spread on it and placed the enticing smorgasbord on the slope above us. The dog would have to go through us to get even a sniff of our lunch.

"What are you doing, Cahill?" Jack queried.

"Oh, I don't want to have to kill this guy's dog," I responded.

I have changed my thoughts on the matter over the years, because now I have this dog. She is a 70 pound Wiemaraner. Her AKC registry name is "Thunderstorm Chaser". We call her Storm. She can run alongside an ATV, pass it, double back, pass it again and so on until the machine runs out of fuel. She goes almost everywhere with me. She loves to fish. The dog actually points fish. Not so much individual fish, but rather where they are holding. I figured this out our first day on the river together. I realized that when she stood stone still with one front leg cocked off the ground, and I put the fly out in front of her; the cast usually resulted in a hook-up. I'm not as smart as she is, nor am I sure how she does it, even though we've been out together dozens upon dozens of times. Oh, I've watched her but I still don't get it. Maybe she sees them. I can't without Polaroid sunglasses, and even then they have to move. I didn't know dogs have Polaroid vision. I don't think they do. So I am left to conclude that she smells them. After all, she is a retriever and tracker with a nose the size of my fist and a vacuum-like airway through it. That's my best guess.

I adopted her when she was about 5 years old. My daughter had taken a position that kept her on the road a lot and she couldn't care for the dog any more. So, like a good daddy, I took the dog—reluctantly, but I took her. It was probably one of the better decisions I have made. She has been an absolute delight and an unwaveringly faithful companion. But I didn't know about the fish thing back then.

Wiemaraners are a shorthair breed and not particularly suited to cold weather, so it was well into her first summer with us before it dawned on me to take her fishing. We went one afternoon to the upper Crystal River, just below the turnoff to Marble, Colorado at a spot that is now called "Storm's Hole". Her first time out was a little trying, but it was a learning experience for us both. She had been to doggy school three times before she actually graduated. This, I found out, is not because she is stupid. It is rather because she is obstinate. She is actually very smart, and she caught on quicker than I had expected.

At first there was a lot of splashing around and running up and down the river bank. I knew that she loved the water because my daughter had told me so, and because I saw how she was as an adolescent on the upper Mississippi around Saint Cloud, Minnesota, where my daughter lived at the time she first got Storm. Back then, my daughter lived on a small lake and had a boat. It was almost impossible to get the dog out of the water. When she became obstreperous she was told to "get in the boat". She would wait for hours in the damn thing before she figured out it wasn't leaving the dock. The point is she loved the water, and it was difficult to keep her out of it at first. But with a little time and a little patience, which is the stuff time is made of; she began to understand what I wanted.

Storm quickly understood that "My Water" meant anything upstream of my position was off limits to her. She got the meaning of "Move Up" quickly, which meant to follow me upstream but stay behind. And "Cross" was something she seemed to know before I would even speak. It was as if she could read me, either by the way I stood or moved. "Find 'em" was a no-brainer for her, and on that command she would begin to search the water for fish. It was truly remarkable, and I hadn't even caught a fish yet.

We began to work well together over the course of that first afternoon, and finally I hooked up with a big fish in a good sized pool of some depth. The instant my line tightened and the rod bent, her ears pricked and she watched my line as it cut back and forth through the water. When the large rainbow broke the surface, she charged in and swam across the pool to fetch it. I had to use my loudest and sternest command to "Back OFF" for fear that she might catch herself on the unoccupied hook of my double fly rig. She instantly swam back to my side, stood on the bank next to me, and shook the water from her coat. I continued to fight the powerful fish, which no doubt was even more frightened by the dog's charge. It broke water again. That was more than Storm could weather. She charged the water again and grabbed the fish. Swimming it back to me, she dropped it in the inch-deep water at my feet. Of course the fish took off into the current of the big pool, but by this time it was so tired that I easily drew it right back in by simply raising the rod. The fight was out of it.

Suddenly this was out of control. It's one thing to have a dog along that points fish, but something altogether different to have one that retrieves them. I had to do something about it and right then. If anybody saw, and anybody was the Game Warden, it would be my ass. If she continued such behavior it could result in injury to her from a hook-and what about the poor fish? It really didn't matter how soft her mouth was. That couldn't be good for the fish. Hell, I'm a catch and release fisherman. Not damaging the fish is the whole idea. All this went through my mind at the speed of light as I reached down to release the spent rainbow.

I wet my hand and coddled the fish onto its back so that it wouldn't struggle. Storm stood at my side, shaking with the prospect of biting it. I held it unhooked, but still upside down, to her nose. She opened her mouth to take it. With my other hand I cuffed her lower jaw clapping it shut.

"No!" I scolded loudly

She backed off a step. When I released the fish she stepped forward and bit the water where the fish had disappeared. As the day wore on she began to understand what it meant to drift, and watched the end of my line float with the current as only a dog can watch something. When the rod bent with the set of the hook, she seemed to know immediately that a fish was on. While I played it she stamped and huffed by my side.

I brought the fish in and repeated the process of unhooking it, while she trembled from anticipation beside me. When I presented the fish to her nose she turned her head away. I lowered the inverted fish to the water, righted and pumped it in the current a few strokes, and it rocketed from my cradled palm. Storm lowered her head and chomped the water several times where the fish had disappeared.

"There," I thought to myself. "Trained".

I'm still not quite sure who was the trainer and who was the trainee. These days we fish together in the same manner. She stands at my side, intently watching my line like no fisherman can. She has taught me the meaning of patience. There's a lot of waiting when you're a dog.

# Drift 17

# The Big Two-Hearted Dutchman

A few times through the course of one's life, someone is encountered who turns into a lifelong friend, and with whom one makes certain passages. I have been lucky in that regard, as I have numerous such friends. Some, too many, have passed. Big Jack was such a man. It seems forever ago that I first encountered him. It was-almost. Thirty five years is a long time. One must reach their 35th birthday before knowing their parents that long. A friend of that many years is indeed a gift.

As a young man, the big Dutchman cut an imposing physical presence. His 6'4" frame and bushy mop of hair, punctuated with eyeglasses and a walrus tusk mustache, gave a misleading impression at first look. Arms that hung down at his sides farther than any I had ever seen, and never seemed to move during the lumbering gait of his walk, led me, at least upon first sight of him, to some incorrect assumptions.

For when he spoke I was entertained and, despite his gangly appearance and odd posture, he possessed the reflexes of a cat.

His height alone drew attention to him, and the rag mop of hair was a signal flag that could not go unnoticed. He was easy to spot in a crowd, but could disappear in a twinkling. The first few times I saw him I could not recall his name and referred to him as "The Big Guy"-a moniker that stuck. I have many memories of Big Jack.

My favorites are the fishing ones. They are the stuff of piscatorial legend. Not because of the fishing, but rather the happenstance of his company. The sight of his immense frame clad in camouflage neoprene waders, head crowned with a pink corduroy ball cap, running down Alaska's Anchor River, hooked into a big Silver Salmon comes to mind. When he set the hook, I noticed the white knob of his fly reel flick off into the turbid water of the little estuary. Like an expectorated molar after a bout of fisticuffs, it had vector and trajectory. Cat-like reflexes or not, he couldn't catch it. Even if he had there was little he could do with. It was lost. And a fly reel without the crank is useless. There was naught to do about it, save what he did.

He danced his way along the sandy bank after the fish as it fled for the ocean, from whence it had just come. As he nimbly moved downstream, he pulled a great length of line in by spreading his long arms. Locking the line in his rod hand, he brought the reel to his mouth and bit the line. He shoved his rod hand out as far as he could reach with the line locked in his teeth, thus gaining another long stroke on the fish. With the line still clenched in his teeth, he reached with his free hand to the extended rod and retrieved yet another stroke on the fish. With the line tight in his hand he brought the rod toward his mouth again and bit the line and so on, all the way to the salt of the Cook Inlet, some hundred yards downstream. His long reach and step aided him greatly in the pursuit. Soon he landed the big Silver at the inlet's edge.

It was angling acumen of a high caliber. A congratulatory murmur of "well done" began to flow through the crowd of 20 or so w'anglers along the little estuary. As he revived and released the fish, the oohs! and ahs! turned to gasps from the meat gatherers.

He rose from the crouch of releasing the fish and surveyed the crowd of w'anglers, who stood silently, lines in hand as the ultimate gesture of courtesy. I watched from across the river as he took in the scene. His meaty hands dangled at his sides on those great long arms. The rod stuck straight out in front of him. His pink hat sat irreverently skewed. As the w'anglers stared at him in silence, he chortled like a tickled kid. And with those long arms hanging straight down and motionless, he crossed the river and headed for camp. It was a great moment.

One September Saturday morning I rousted him early to fish Kokanee Salmon on the East River on the south side of Kebler Pass, below Crested Butte. I left his place in Aspen for mine in Carbondale, with his promise to purchase the provisions and be no more than an hour or so behind. By the third hour I was getting pissed. Then he showed up in the huge white pickup and topper shell that was his uniform. He was sorry, and it took some time to get the groceries, and he'd never go to that market again.

I called him on his tardiness and busted his chops a little by virtue of a friend's right. He tossed my castigation aside with his usual caustic quip or insult—or both.

Actually, it all worked out quite well. We were able to fish Anthracite Creek before dark and camp at Erickson Springs. We decided to make the Kebler Pass drive in the morning. There was plenty of time the next day for catching Kokes. He prepared an excellent meal that evening. After dinner, while he tidied the kitchen gear, I pulled out my fly tying kit and began to set up on the camp table. As I sat in the chill of a September evening under the glare of a gas lantern, with my back to the fire, rummaging a bag for feathers, he disappeared into the blackness of his pickup bed, parked some yards away from the table. I could hear the clatter of gear being moved under the topper shell, and then a cab door opened and closed. I gave it no more thought and began to tie a fly.

From the pitch black that surrounds any light in the woods, he appeared without warning. Not even the size thirteen boots that shod him made a sound as he approached. He spoke my name and startled me from the wrapping of a fly I was tying. All of a sudden he was just there, next to me.

I looked up from the vise to see him holding a large chocolate sheet cake on a thin aluminum pan. It was plastered with white icing. It was the kind from a supermarket bakery. He plopped the large confection down on the table under the lantern's hiss. The table shook and the thud it made hinted at its density. On the top were some words written in green icing. I read it twice to make sure. "Johnny—Good Luck Fishing" was squirted across it.

"That's what took me so long," he said. "Just when I told the lady what to write there was a problem with a KID birthday cake. And you know me and kid problems. I did the shopping and got beer and she still wasn't done with it. It took forever."

We had cake and beer for desert. It was good.

The next day we passed that big ass cake back and forth between trucks all day long. He didn't want it in his truck.

"It's your cake," he announced.

"I don't want that in my truck; besides you have all the other food," I argued.

"It's still your cake," was all he would say.

I must have stuck that thing in his truck four or five times throughout the day, only to find it back in mine as many. By the time we were done, frosting was on all my gear. When I emptied my truck at home, I found the cake neatly hidden under my waders. Even though that was many years ago, I still have those waders and that frosting is indelibly pressed into the weave of the fabric.

I met him in Alamosa for a fall jaunt one October. We spent the night there before heading south to the Conejos River. I really love the Conejos River valley; it is a beautiful place. Along its entire length from Antonito to Platoro at the river's headwaters, there are few inhabitants. The Conejos is to the Rio Grande what the Roaring Fork is to the Colorado. Mostly the river runs its course through National Forest. There are a few scattered in holds along its lower course but the river, above where the state highway turns south over Cumbres Pass to Chama, New Mexico, is heaven for fly fishermen. I had booked a cabin at the Rocky Mountain Lodge. It's one of those yesteryear Colorado getaways boasting a plethora of fine old cabins, some from the late 1800's and some from the 1940's. We stayed in one with the date of 1890 carved into the lintel above the door. The lodge owner said it was the original homestead cabin.

We checked in and began unloading to the cabin, when the resident dog came over to greet us. I'm not sure of his breed, but he was a shorthair variety with a bobtail, the kind of bob that left no tail. Big Jack started in on the poor animal immediately.

"Hey dude, what happened to your tail?" he chided. "Man you look stupid without a tail, dude."

The dog wiggled his rear end all the harder and issued one of those snorts that only happy dogs can make. This delighted Big Jack, and he continued his merciless teasing with other inquiries about the mutt's tail as he scratched behind its ears. It became the morning and evening ritual. The dog waited for us in the morning, and came running from wherever he spent the day to greet us each afternoon. It was quite comical to see the little mutt and the giant Dutchman interact.

Of course, in October the Conejos valley is vacant except for the hunters who stay well off the river. Once again we had a place to our selves. It was a joy. Above the confluence with its South Fork there is a section called the Palisades. It is a walled canyon section and only accessible during low water times; generally that means Spring or Fall. October was perfect for accessing it. We started there after spending the early part of the frosty morning drinking coffee and helping the dog look for his tail.

Making our way up the river, we came upon a large wild raspberry patch right on the water's edge. Big Jack was ahead of me and continued upstream as I ambled around the perimeter of the patch. Something wasn't right. I stopped to look at the patch for moment. The berries were gone. I mean all gone. Not even a shriveled or deformed one was to be found. It seemed odd to me, but I continued to the water and started to fish. Big Jack fished about fifty feet upstream of me, mumbling something about my aroma.

"What the hell is he grousing about?" I thought.

I lost that thought when a large, healthy rainbow that had never been hooked ripped me. Sometimes you can just tell by the way the fish reacts. Big Jack moved back downstream to w'angle.

"Nice fish", he congratulated.

He stood behind me with his nose stuck in the air sniffing me. It was a little distracting and I glowered over my shoulder at him once during the fight with the powerful fish. I drew the fish in the last few yards, but it saw our feet in the water and ripped me again, taking the line to the other side of the river. The reel sang that whiny tune all fly fisherman dance to. Even palming the rim drag did little to slow it, and as the line grew in weight due to its length, I felt sure to lose the fish. Somehow, I kept a tight line and drew it back across the river. This time it was spent. I worked quickly to release it. Jack leaned down to look at it while I removed the hook with the spent fish still in the water and sniffed me again. I pumped the fish a few times to revive it. It shot from my hands and disappeared into the textured water. When I stood, Big Jack was still sniffing me.

"What in the "cornbread" hell is wrong with you?" I demanded.

"Nothing," he said and started to move upstream again.

We moved upstream to the approximate spot where he had stood when I hooked the rainbow and he had mumbled. He stopped and turned with an inquisitive look knitting his brow.

"What?" I quizzed.

"Don't you smell that?"

I moved up through the ankle-deep water to his position and sniffed the air. I could smell it. The odor was rank and pervasive.

"That's gotta' be your upper lip," I quipped.

I half recognized the odor but I couldn't quite place it. We moved upstream a few yards and the odor dissipated. There at the entry to the Palisades, where the cliffs close in on the river, I saw tracks leading up to a small opening above the fine scree at the base of the cliff. One of those little lights went on.

"What do you think made these?" I asked Big Jack.

I inspected the tracks closest to us at the bottom of the sandy scree-definitely bear. I said so, standing up from my crouch.

"That's what the stink is," I suggested.

"You mean from that cave?"

"No. Somewhere from inside all that brush we just passed. I knew I recognized that odor. There's a bear in that brush. Did you notice the raspberry patch was bare? I think it's sleeping off a berry glut in that thick brush we just passed, or it's watching us," I surmised in a whisper.

I signed for us to be quiet and pointed Big Jack to the other side of the river. We quietly made our way downstream before we spoke aloud again.

"That was close. If we could smell it—it was close."

Big Jack went a little green to match the turmoil I felt welling in my gut. We decided to forego the Palisades section for the day, agreeing to try it from the top end access later. We figured the bear was probably not working it, as there wasn't really anything along the length of that walled section that a bear would be interested in. It was reasonable to assume that its range was more likely downstream of the den.

Our best option seemed to be the South Fork and we made our way downstream on the main river to the trail. It was a relief to be away from the bear, and our mood lightened as we made our way the mile and a half trail to the South Fork. It was our first time on the South Fork of the Conejos and we were pleasantly astounded to come upon an ancient grove of aspen trees. Some were the diameter of a pickup truck tire, truly big trees. It was as if we had entered another time, when only Native Americans and wildlife roamed the valley. Some of the big trees had dates and names carved into them. They were unreadable until I stepped back far enough to compensate for the distortion the trees' growth had put on the letters and numerals. Dates from the late 1800's were clearly visible. What a magnificent grove it is. That sight alone was worth the drive. Big Jack and I clasped hands and tried to reach around the biggest of the giants. We could not, even with the advantage of his great long arms.

We couldn't fish the South Fork, for it was raging and not crossable. I thought this a bit odd, as the main river was in fine shape. On the walk back to the truck I understood, when a horrific thunderstorm came over the ridges from where the South Fork began. The lighting was blinding and the thunder deafening. We had to take cover under a deep cut bank of the old channel where the river had long since departed for a new course. We waited a good hour for the storm to pass before making the last leg across an open meadow to the truck.

Back at the cabin that night Big Jack spent some time helping the dog look for his tail. The next day it snowed and we left for home.

The cake that wouldn't go away

# Drift 18

# Parshall Red Tide

The last trip I took with Big Jack was to the Williams Fork of the Colorado, which empties into that great and historic western waterway at the small burg of Parshall. Now that's an interesting name and I'm only speculating as to its origins, but this is what I think. The little hamlet in just about halfway between Kremmling and Hot Sulphur Springs on U.S. Highway 40, which runs along the upper Colorado. My theory is that some cowpoke of earlier times, when that part of the country was even less populated than it is now, was on his way from Kremmling to Hot Sulphur Springs when his horse gave out and he had to spend the night there. Thus making it only Parshall the distance to his destination. Or, he turned off to ride up the Williams Fork enticed by the beauty of the little valley, or maybe just to check for strays. He liked the spot and was Parshall to it. Either one works. And it's the best explanation I can conjure to the origin of the name.

I spent the first day driving from Olathe to Granby via Grand Junction to pick up Mudge at Walker Field. He flew in from California especially for this post Labor Day trip. We drove all day to the town of Granby, where we booked some motel rooms for the rest of the Gang, which included Big Jack, Stumpy and Spoons. We all agreed to meet early the next morning at the parking lot of the Williams Fork access.

Mudge and I reached the lot as close to on time as a fishing appointment requires, and Stumpy rolled up in his truck within moments of our arrival. He spent the night up on Williams Fork Reservoir. The Williams Fork was dammed at some point, forming a large reservoir, and as usual the resulting tail water became a prolific fishery. We leisurely got ready, hoping that our slow pace would allow the final pair, Big Jack and Spoons to arrive before we made the two mile walk to the fabulous little river. At last ready, there was naught to do but wait or leave.

"Let's go. Those two can catch up with us. I've been impatient long enough," Mudge complained and started out across the long alluvial bench to the Williams Fork. Stumpy and I followed. The bench is like the brim of a large Stetson, with a hill around which it wraps as the crown. There's a funny thing about the Williams Fork. It cannot be seen from anywhere in the area until one gets right on top of it. But once the two mile walk is trudged, and one reaches the end of the hat brim, a stunning surprise is just below your feet. The tiniest little valley, lush and green in the warmer months and brilliantly colored in the fall, presents itself as if by some magician's trick. It is one of those sweet spots. I also am a little Parshall to it.

The tail water between the dam and the confluence with the Colorado is only about a mile and half in length, but there is so much packed into that short distance that at times I have found it hard to fish. Sitting and looking seems to be what the place was made for.

We fished the day up and down its length and even spent a few drifts on the Colorado itself. The fishing was slow. Whirling disease had taken its toll here, too, but it made little difference to us. We could not see our desks and there is no cell phone reception, not that any of us brought one. I never bring a cell phone fishing, but I have heard them ring on certain other rivers. Just the thought of a place where the damn things don't work was a relief, and worth spending the day in, fish or not.

By lunch, Big Jack and Spoons had not shown themselves. We fished a few more passes along the river's length before making the walk back to the trucks. We found them sitting in lawn chairs on the shady side of their truck, drinking beer.

"What the hell happened to you guys?" I asked

"We took the wrong turn on Highway 9 and ended up back in Dillon this morning," Big Jack admitted. "We didn't get here 'till about 2 o'clock."

"Where the hell IS the river?" Spoons asked sheepishly. "We walked out there a ways but I didn't see it."

They only made it Parshall the way.

We spent another day poking around the upper Colorado and some of the creeks that feed it. Our last night at dinner we decided to try the Colorado River at Yarmony Crossing, a few miles upstream of State Bridge. It was on our way back and seemed a good afternoon break on our 4 hour ride home. But first we spent the morning messing around a little creek I knew of, just to see what would happen. When lunch called, we were in Kremmling and stopped for a hearty one at a local eatery. That's when the thunderstorm hit with a vengeance. By the time we finished lunch the rain was still coming down, and knowing Colorado weather, we decided to have another beer while we waited for the storm to pass, which it finally did two beers later.

We gassed up and headed south for the Trough Road that connects Colorado Highway #9 outside of Kremmling to Colorado Highway #131 at State Bridge on the Colorado River. It's one of the short cuts I often take. The ride along the north end of the Piney Ridge and the feet of the Gore Range is as scenic as any in the west. Riding the lonesome sage high above the river affords a view that cannot be found in many places. One can see the Gore and Elk Ranges, and across the canyon there are huge ranches that speak to the solitude and remoteness of the land. In some places the view of Gore Canyon and the river below is a snippet of another canyon made by the Colorado, far to the south in the arid Arizona high country, and there are several good places to stop and fish like Radium and Pumphouse.

When we reached the Trough Road, I stopped to engage the front hubs of my faithful F-250. We were beginning to catch up to the storm, and I knew we would be glad of the security that 4 wheel drive gave us while traveling the high dirt road in the rain. Every pickup owner knows that they ride better even on a dry dirt road in 4 wheel. At the top of the hill that climbs to the high country from the Blue River side at Kremmling, we caught the storm. It was even worse there than it had been back down in town. At least it seemed that way, maybe because we were in the middle of nowhere at the time. Where the road affords a view of the river below above the Pumphouse turnoff, we could see the river was red. The storm runoff was carrying loads of red silt into it. I knew it wouldn't be long until the red tide reached Yarmony, and the fishing would be pointless. I was sure we wouldn't be fishing the Colorado.

At Yarmony, where the road crosses the river and the DW & RG Railroad has a siding and switching yard, the umber turbidity of the river was only a harbinger. As I climbed the hill out of Yarmony, I could see the others coming down the upriver side and crossing the bridge. We rolled down the State Bridge side of the little knoll that separates it from Yarmony, and parked the truck at a pull off where the Trough Road intersects the Highway #131 river bridge. The others caught us moments later.

"What the hell, Cahill, I thought we were gonna' fish Yarmony?" Big Jack groused as he approached my truck.

"Did you see the river back there?" I asked with a bit of tone in my voice.

"It wasn't that dirty," he said.

"It will be," I assured him and the others.

We walked out to the highway and sat on the bridge rails. The river was a wonderful jade hue, which it often is.

"So what's the deal?" Jack asked with a bit of disdain.

"Just watch," was all I needed to say.

Slowly but relentlessly the water began to turn color. At first it became a dingy brown, but minute by minute the shade deepened.

Soon the red tide made the corner around the little knoll, just upstream off our location. By the time it passed under the bridge, it was the color of adobe mixed with oxblood, and moments later it went crimson. I had often seen the Colorado run red below Glenwood Springs some 40 miles downstream after a good rain. But now I understood why. Even though the fishing had been slow, I considered it a great trip if only by virtue of that sight. I shall be forever Parshall to that memory.

# Drift 19

# Net Boy

All through my childhood I was privy to Jack's penchant for assigning monikers to people. He did it as a matter of fact, without malice and with more relish than a man should enjoy over such things. It tickled him endlessly to come up with a good one, and he usually addressed the person by this nickname no matter what they thought. Most liked it—a few did not. He really didn't care either way. If he liked you, he gave you a good one, or at least a funny one. If he didn't like you it was usually a demeaning one. He didn't care. He just called it like he saw it.

A good example from my early teens was a guy who lived across the street and mowed his lawn with earmuffs on his head. Not the kind of ear protectors that airport tarmac workers or target shooters wear, but rather the old fashioned fuzzy ones on a coiled steel band that are actually ear warmers. The man's name was Stan. Jack referred to him as "Stan-Stan the Ear Muff Man", a moniker of dubious distinction.

There was a next door neighbor named, "Jerstead" whom Jack called "Jerkstead", because he was one.

Just before I graduated from high school, we lived in an old farmhouse that was the original homestead around which a new housing development had been built. On the farm was an old three-sided loafing shed with an unlevel dirt floor. One corner of the floor was so out of level that I could scoot under the wall of the shed. Jack decided to build a forge in the shed, and wanted me to haul some dirt in to level the floor and close the big gap under the back wall. He showed me a spot from where he wanted the dirt taken. We began digging and wheel barrowing the dirt to the shed floor. Soon a man came out from one of the new subdivision houses and complained that we were digging a hole on his property. Jack argued with him for a while, but the man would not relent and threatened to call the police. Jack made me move all the dirt back into the man's hole. Later he had the property surveyed and found that we were actually digging on our property, but it was too late. I had already completed the job with dirt from another location. He showed the guy the survey stakes—and metaphorically made the guy eat dirt when he named him "Hole Boy." He called the man that to his face the entire time we lived in that house.

I had a college buddy who made the mistake of coming to visit me at home one summer break. He was tall and sported shoulder length blonde hair with a few feathers tied in it. He wore hippie beads around his neck and was fond of leather vests and moccasins. Jack instantly hung the moniker of "Yellow Knife" on him for his Indian-like garb.

That poor slob has been "Yellow Knife" for the last thirty-five years, despite his hair cut and business suit.

After a lifetime of fishing hundreds of rivers and lakes, tying and losing thousands of flies, and making hundreds of thousands of casts with millions of steps between them, I took some rare opportunities to fish with my first fishing buddy as I entered middle age and he started retirement. They amounted to only a few times, but they were of such a special nature to me that they stand out as significant.

In the first year of his retirement Jack bought a monstrous fifth-wheel travel trailer. He and Mom spent almost a year roaming the country in search of their retirement dream. Before finding that place, they stopped in Colorado to attend my younger brother's wedding. I knew Jack wanted me to take him fishing. So I arranged a day on the Frying Pan River.

He arrived from his campsite up the Crystal River at my house in Carbondale about midmorning the day before the wedding. We took my faithful F-250 to the Gold Medal catch and release tail water on the Frying Pan below Reudi Dam. Of course Jack knew where I was taking him from all the phone conversations about fishing, and he was like a kid on his way to Disneyland during the ride up from Carbondale.

Arriving at the river, we found it packed with fisherman. I felt a little disappointed for placing him in a combat fishing situation. It was not the scene I had envisioned, much the way that life itself seems to work out. But he was game and more interested in the river than its occupants. I found a good place to park where we could have a little space to ourselves and began the process I had done so many times before. Except this time I had to do it for Jack as well as myself. Our roles from my childhood were suddenly reversed. Getting the neoprene waders on him was the toughest part, rather like trying to put toothpaste back in the tube. He insisted on rigging his own rod, but the tiny flies that work best on the Frying Pan were too small, and the tippet required too fine, for him to tie on the leader. I let him fiddle with it while I rigged myself. When finished, I took his rod and tucked it under my armpit.

"You don't have to do that," he said while I started tying on the spider web that is 6X tippet and then a little #20 fly to its end.

"I think I can do this, considering all the times you did it for me," I told him.

"Yeah, I guess you owe me a couple," he agreed

"I'd say more than a couple."

We laughed as he recalled aloud some of the birds' nests and tree snags he'd untangled for me over the years of my childhood, tedious jobs that took away his fishing time and about which he never complained. I pinched a small BB split shot on the leader above the tippet knot and tiny fly.

"Here you go," I said, handing him the rod.

"That was quick," he said.

"Yeah, well I've only done it a few times. Hang on a minute while I get a net. Then let's cross the bridge and walk downstream a little," I suggested.

I rummaged my fishing gear box and pack, but I couldn't find my good cotton net and had to settle for an old wide mouth nylon one that

I kept in the truck for big Salmon and Bass. I hooked the bungee cord lanyard to the ring on the nape of my vest. We set off for the flatter, more negotiable water below the bridge.

There, I showed Jack the basics of nymphing and was pleasantly surprised to see him hook up with a few big Frying Pan Rainbows; made fat and healthy from a steady diet of Mysis shrimp. The fish took the fly with the gentlest of mouth, and a few misses occurred before he got the hang of their almost imperceptible take. Soon he realized that a stop in the drift meant a fish was holding the fly. As we worked our way upstream toward the bridge, he started to hook up every cast or two. I netted his catch with the big nylon salmon net. Holding the net with the fish in the water, I let Jack release them. He was tickled.

By the time we covered the few hundred yards to the bridge, Jack had landed about a dozen fish and was actually spent from it all. I suggested lunch on the tailgate of my truck and he gladly agreed.

"That water is a little cold. My feet are numb," he half complained about the 50 degree water coming from the tailrace.

"They'll warm with a little sun and lunch," I assured him. "Then we can fish the upper section above the bridge. There're a few really good holes up there."

We finished lunch and Jack pulled his video camera from the truck cab. His feet had warmed up.

"I want to get some shots of you fishing," he said.

We walked several hundred yards along the south side road, with the willows turning yellow between us and the river, to a spot above the bridge that I knew as Two Rocks. Here the willows opened for a bit to allow access to the river. I stepped down the bank into the water, going in only about ankle deep. Jack stood several feet above on the bank with his video camera at the ready. I waved to a fisherman across the river and just upstream. He looked my way but ignored my greeting. Several other fishermen were also upstream on my side and I greeted them with the usual inquiry to their luck. They expressed their disappointment.

I unhooked the tiny #20 Quill Midge from the keeper on the rod handle, pulled some line out, and began to cast upstream, drifting the channel a rod's length from my feet. I hooked and landed a little Cutbow, and released it by clenching the leader just above the split shot with my rod hand, leaving the other free to remove the barbless hook from the small fish while it was still in the water, never touching it. Jack filmed it and commented for the video audience how I had removed some river moss from the tippet knot before releasing the fish. This sparked a little chuckle from the other fishermen on my side of the river. Soon I had landed and released six or so fish of varying size and they moved down to inquire what fly I used.

I chatted with them, showing them the little Quill Midge. They hadn't seen such a fly before. I pulled my fly box out and handed one to each of them. They were immensely grateful and began removing the dry flies they had been casting. While they sat on the bank changing their rigs, we chatted as I continued to fish. The fisherman across the river only fifty feet away appeared sullen, and continued unsuccessfully to ply the water around him. He was the only one in the immediate vicinity who hadn't asked me about my choice of fly. I could smell a little resentment on the breeze coming down the river. The sour aroma was but a hint of things to come.

As I chatted with the guys sitting behind me on the bank, I felt that gentle stop of my drift that only fishing the leader will allow the angler to detect. I ignored the chatter behind me, and raised the rod vigorously until the line was taut and the tip bent slightly. Instantly the little bit of slack line floating at my feet burned through my free hand until it was paid out and began to whine off the reel. I knew what was on the end of my line—a big fish. Only big fish take line as this one did. It torpedoed downstream pulling my rod almost parallel with the water surface. I knew the line would go static and pull the hook out if I didn't get the rod tip up by showing the fish the butt. I let line out under a controlled drag with my free hand on the palming rim of the reel, at the same time pointing the rod butt at the fish to arc the rod, thus putting its power against the fish and taking the stress off the tiny fly and gossamer tippet. I did all this while moving downstream, trying to keep the fish as close to right angles to the line and rod as possible. With the fish on the reel, I was able to stop its downstream run and as is often the case, when one direction doesn't free them, they try another.

When the big fish turned and ran straight for me the line went slack and I was sure to lose it. Frantically, I stripped line back in with my free hand, trying desperately to keep some rod tension on the fish while racing it back upstream to where Jack and the w'anglers stood. By the time I caught up, the fish saw my boot shod feet and tore across the river straight for the lone angler on the opposite bank. I let it take the line with a minimum of palm drag applied, for now it was swimming against the current.

It breeched and tail walked, shaking its head wildly. At last all could see that it was a truly big Rainbow, in the five pound range. This brought some comments from the w'anglers behind me, and Jack laughed aloud. The fish rubbed its head and side in the gravel bottom of the shallow water on the other side of the current. It looked like it was making a spawning red, but it was really trying to get the hook out. I'd seen this before; in fact I've seen fish run straight into the opposite bank or a big rock in the same effort. Often they are successful.

After the aerial and the rubbing, the fish parked itself within a few feet of the opposite bank angler. The guy kept fishing the water right where my quarry had come to rest. I thought it a bit odd that he didn't reel in or at least take a step back. After all, that would have been proper fishing etiquette. I ignored the obvious slight and pulled the fish toward me by alternately raising the rod and cranking the reel on the down stroke. Even though the fish was spent it still took some effort to bring it back across the current. The big fish gave one final tug and then all but swam to me.

With the big Rainbow so close, I realized that my usual technique of clenching the leader in my rod hand against the handle and removing the hook with my free hand wouldn't work. The fish was too big. If it thrashed and released itself, I would probably get a hook driven in my hand by the recoil of the rod; our worse yet might catch the fish again in an eye or gill. I reached for the big nylon Salmon net hanging from the nape of my vest, netted it and held the big Rainbow with the net, still in the water, for Jack to see. He was rolling the video camera.

Congratulations came from the w'anglers behind me on the bank. But from across the river came something all together different.

"Hey! You're not supposed to use that kind of net on these fish," the lone angler across from me chided. I ignored him but the guy continued his castigation.

"Those nets damage the fish. You're supposed to use cotton nets."

"Is that so?" I responded, trying my best to maintain my cool. I felt a little guilty but I had only brought the net in case Jack needed some help with a large fish. I really didn't intend to use it as a matter of course.

"Yeah! And it's guys like you that are ruining this river," he continued. That was enough. I wasn't about to be badgered by this guy.

"How about you mind your own business?" I demanded.

"You're killing fish," he accused.

As the argument progressed, the w'anglers behind me moved off the slope and ascended the bank to stand next to Jack, who still had the video camera rolling. I continued to release the big Rainbow, keeping the net in the water while I removed the tiny Quill Midge from its jaw. I wet my free hand and grabbed the lunker by the tail, then slid the big net from under it. A few pumps back and forth in the current it revived. Bolting away, it actually displayed one more aerial leap before it swam out of sight.

"That fish looked OK to me," I insisted loudly so my voice was sure to carry across the river. I was starting to lose my patience. I knew this could well be one of the last times I would fish with Jack and I was sure it was the only time I would be able to get him on the Frying Pan. It was an important day for both of us that didn't need to be sullied by some jerk's interference in matters that weren't his concern.

"Don't worry—you killed it," he insisted with an overly snide tone. "Those nylon nets remove the protective oil from the fish. Plus they scratch the skin and that lets parasites attack. Don't worry-you killed it."

The deep well of my patience was dry and dusty. Who did this guy think he was? I couldn't believe I was involved in a confrontation over a net.

"Look, pal," I said while hooking my fly to the rod keeper. "You just saw me land and release six fish without even touching them. And the only reason I used the net was because the fish was so big. Bigger, I might add, than anything I've seen you catch—which is none. And if you think my net did any more damage to that fish than it did to itself trying to rub my hook out on the bottom—you're nuts. I know you saw that because it happened right at your feet. And beyond that, I haven't seen any nylon that absorbs anything, whereas cotton absorbs everything. So I think you're out of line and if I hear one more word out of you—I'm coming across and we're gonna' dance. What are you any way—the Fish Police?"

He wouldn't shut up about the net or my abuse of the fish and continued his tirade. I turned and tossed my rod to Jack standing four feet above me on the bank. With my favorite 3 weight rod out of my hands and safe, I started to cross the river. I heard Jack from the bank above say, "Oh shit—Johnny no!" The guy began reeling in and backing up at the same time. He fell over trying get out of the water and landed on his butt with an audible thud, which is where I intended to put him once I gained the opposite bank. I was too slow (intentionally), and he ran off through the willow thicket behind him.

I regained my self control when I saw him humiliate himself, and decided he wasn't worth the bush whack through those willows I'd have to endure to catch him. Besides I had already put him on his butt without even touching him—sort of the same way I had landed the first few fish. I didn't really want to catch him. I just wanted him to shut up.

As I turned to regain the bank and take my rod back from Jack, the w'anglers applauded me.

"I thought he'd never leave," one of them said, and we all laughed.

"Who the hell was that guy?" another asked.

From behind the video camera stuck to his face Jack said, "That was Net Boy."

We laughed like hell all the way home. The next day Jack presented me with a copy of the video tape. He had captured the entire incident. He even put titles and credits into it.

"Fishing the Frying Pan"—staring "Colorado Johnny"—with a special appearance by "Net Boy."

I still have that tape.

# Drift 20

# The Last Cast

Not long after we met Net Boy on the Frying Pan, Jack and Mom found their retirement dream on Florida's west coast at the hamlet of Estero, between Naples and Fort Myers. They bought a nice little house on the fifth green of a golf course. It took me another few years to make it down there. Over those intervening years I had been to Alaska a number of times. And of course Jack and I had discussed the trips extensively on the telephone. Now he wanted me to come to Florida to fish. I managed to take some time from my business and left the high country behind for few weeks of sun, sand, seafood and golf with my bride. I also brought my big water rods and fly tying gear.

What I didn't know was that he meant only me about the fishing. Life had taken its inexorable toll on him as it does with all of us, so he wasn't the agile and durable fisherman he once had been. Arthritis plagued him to the point that he couldn't sit or stand for long periods and had to break up his day by alternately doing both. So spending the day in a boat was out, as was traipsing shorelines the way we had so often done together in my youth.

Of course, he had other motives for me to visit beyond fishing. I had become an accomplished furniture and cabinet maker over the years. He managed to conjure a plethora of jobs for me to do around the new house, which he had barely been able to start let alone complete.

We built a large set of closets at the back end of the garage, with deep shelves and special little boxes attached to the inside of the doors. He badly needed some organization applied to his two-car garage/shop. It really wasn't a garage anymore. There were too many woodworking tools, both hand and floor, to call it that. A bicycle couldn't find a place to rest in it. Thinking back I can't remember a single house from my childhood in which Jack used the garage for a car.

"Worst waste of space there is," he often proclaimed. "A vehicle that can't live outside isn't worth having."

It's not surprising to me that I've adopted the same attitude toward garages. Anyway, we spent a few days fixing up his with a lot of racks, shelves, bins and closets. After a few days of eating sawdust, we moved to the yard for the more mundane and less skilled tasks on his list. We (I) built planter boxes, trimmed his citrus and palm trees and fixed the pool cover. Then he put me in the oven of an attic to run audio and TV cables for all his electronic gear. I spent the first week catching him up. He complained that I worked him too hard, but in fact it was the other way around.

Then he released me to spend some time with my bride. We golfed and walked the beach. Mostly we stuffed ourselves with seafood. There's a great seafood place, called Rhodes, on the Bonita Beach road serving the best crab cake subs south of the Chesapeake. Those we took to go and ate on the beach. After a long walk on the surf line, she and I had a bucket of steamers and beers at one of the many crab shacks on the water's edge. We spent the next few days passing the time in this manner, returning to the folks' house for dinner.

Jack surprised me one day with a guided bass fishing trip on Lake Okeechobee. Somehow, he had found a retired schoolteacher with a bass boat who guided for a very reasonable fee. Of course he couldn't go for various reasons, but mostly because of the arthritis.

It wasn't the best fishing day I ever had. The weather was unseasonably cold for Florida, and even more so, on the big lake. Okeechobee is not very deep, so cold air temperatures affect the water temperature dramatically. The bass were hunkered down and uncooperative. Nonetheless, I managed to skunk my guide with my 8-weight Bass rod and a few hair body flies I had picked up along the way. I caught three decent Large Mouth Bass, once the lake warmed a little under the Florida sun. The day before, Jack and I took a ride to fishing shop he knew of and I augmented my boxes with a few local patterns. One in particular was so enticing that I couldn't resist purchasing it. The pattern is a Rainbow Trout tied in a loudmouth style, with a flat front. It is designed to be used as a top water fly and strip jerked across the surface much like a standard cork popper, often used for pan fish and bass. The damn thing cost me eight bucks. Flies of such a nature become investments rather than a casual purchase. On the lake my willpower failed me, for I had to try it out. It lived up to its name. The sound it made when jerked across the water was astounding—a true loud mouth. Even my guide was taken aback by the gurgling chirp it made. Thank God I didn't catch anything on it or it might have been ruined by a big, aggressive bass. It sits in my investment fly box now, waiting to become an antique along with a lot of other gear I have acquired over the years.

The fact is that day on the big lake was a bit melancholy for me. It wasn't the poor fishing or the cold weather that sank my spirits, but rather Jack's absence. I made the best of the situation, for I knew it was something that I was not likely to do again. But frankly I was glad when the day ended. At home that night I gave my best impersonation of an ebullient fisherman who had just spent a wonderful day catching and releasing his quarry. Jack bought it and was never the wiser.

"I missed you out there, Jackie." By then I had taken to calling him Jackie. "It wasn't quite the same without you," I admitted.

"Yeah, I wish I could have seen you skunk the guide," he gleamed. Knowing about that seemed to be enough for him. It wasn't for me.

The weather warmed substantially over the following days, and Jack seemed to regain some of his former mobility, and with that came his old charming demeanor. We kids used to joke that even under the worst circumstances he was always Mr. Personality. We took a few rides around the area to see the sights, while my wife spent her days visiting and sunning by the pool with mom. It was good to be with Jack. I felt like in the old days when I was a kid.

It was during one of those little jaunts that we passed a large county park with a decent lake in the middle.

"Jackie, you think there's any fish in that?" I wondered aloud.

"Seems to be fish is just about everything around here. You wanna' give it a try?"

"Sure. What's the worst that could happen?" I kidded.

"Get eaten by a gator, I guess," he allowed.

The next day after household chores and lunch, Jack and I went to the park. I took only a 6-weight and my vest. Wading was not an option. I also slung a folding lawn chair over my shoulder so that Jack could sit when he tired. I worked the water from the shore and he sat in the lawn chair. The fishing was fair. I caught a few Large Mouth on the surface, with poppers. He took a few turns with the fly rod while I sat in the lawn chair, just like the old days in Utah, except for the lawn chair. He caught and released a few Bass also. It was good to see. He liked it immensely.

We talked and reminisced about all the trips we had taken together. He recounted them all, even the skiing.

He started reminiscing. "Remember the time at Glen Canyon when it snowed and collapsed the tent? You were pretty young back then and—well I wonder if you remember any of those. Like the times on Lake Champlain in the little boat. How about the trip where that big pike took the bluegill off my line, and Pip cooked and ate all the fish on beach before your mom and I got cleaned up and came back down from the cabin. Boy, she was pissed at him for that."

"I remember it all Jackie, every cast."

It was all I could say, stifling a tear. I knew then what this meant. He knew as well. We were fishing our last day together. We talked about it all as we made our way around the lake shore. Stopping at a likely spot, I handed him the rod and unfolded the lawn chair. I sat with my legs stretched out and looked at him

"Your turn." I told him.

# Reeling In

Not long after that last cast I received a call from my little sister telling me that Jack was hospitalized in Fort Meyers, and on life support. I caught the first plane I could get on out of Aspen and made the sad journey to Florida. It was the longest flight I have ever taken. My sister picked me up at the airport about midnight. The next day our two brothers flew in.

We kids and Mom met with the doctors and got the bad news; he wasn't coming out of it. With no hope for a recovery and his DNR in hand, we met the family priest at the hospital to disconnect his life support and administer his last rites. With his wife and all his children at his side and his hand in mine, Jack left on his never ending fishing trip.

Fishing is a little different for me these days. It has taken some time for me to realize why. It wasn't until I reached home one day after a particularly good outing on Anthracite Creek at the bottom end of the Raggeds Wilderness that I understood. That evening while preparing dinner, I picked up the phone and began dialing that old number. The one I had dialed so many times before. I caught myself in mid dial and put the phone back in its cradle.

"Who were you calling?" my bride asked as she passed through the kitchen to the laundry room with an armload of linens.

"Just an old friend." I said.

"You hung up kind of quick. Wasn't he there?"

"No he isn't. I forgot he's on a trip."

# About the Author

J. Wilfred Cahill is Real Estate Broker with fifty years of lake and stream fly fishing under his belt. He lives with his family in southwest Colorado above the banks of the historic Uncompahgre River. He spends his time gardening, woodworking, chasing his toddling grandson and of course fishing with Jack.

Also by J. Wilfred Cahill with Malcolm Smith

"I Never Liked Those C-130's Anyway"

The riotous tale of a legendary Coast Guard aviator